A Cotswold Christmas

Compiled by John Hudson

A Budding Book

First published in 1988 by Alan Sutton Publishing Limited,
an imprint of Sutton Publishing Limited
Phoenix Mill · Thrupp · Stroud · Gloucestershire

This edition first published in 1998 by Budding Books,
an imprint of Sutton Publishing Limited

A catalogue record for this book is available from the
British Library

ISBN 1-84015-094-7

Cover illustration: Christmas Visitors Stirring the Pudding,
*by Frederick Hardy (Christies, London; photograph The Bridgeman
Art Library)*

Typeset in Garamond 12/13.
Typesetting and origination by
Sutton Publishing Limited.
Printed in Great Britain by
WBC Ltd, Bridgend.

from

Cider with Rosie

LAURIE LEE

This first extract from the most beautifully written and justly celebrated Cotswold memoir takes us back to the early 1920s, when Slad's feudal past still had a bearing on village life. The book's charm and wistful appeal lie in its account of the dying of the old ways, which coincided closely with the author's growth to manhood.

The week before Christmas, when snow seemed to lie thickest, was the moment for carol-singing; and when I think back to those nights it is to the crunch of snow and to the lights of the lanterns on it. Carol-singing in my village was a special tithe for the boys, the girls had little to do with it. Like hay-making, blackberrying, stone clearing and wishing-people-a-happy-Easter, it was one of our seasonal perks.

By instinct we knew just when to begin it; a day too soon and we should have been unwelcome, a day too late and we should have received lean looks from people whose bounty was already exhausted. When the true moment came, exactly balanced, we recognised it and were ready.

So as soon as the wood had been stacked in the oven to dry for the morning fire, we put on our scarves and went out through the streets, calling loudly between our hands, till the

1

Carol singers in Bisley around the time of the First World
War.

Clearing snow in Bisley after the huge falls of March 1916.

various boys who knew the signal ran out from their houses to join us.

One by one they came stumbling over the snow, swinging their lanterns around their heads, shouting and coughing horribly.

'Coming carol-barking then?'

We were the Church Choir, so no answer was necessary. For a year we had praised the Lord out of key, and as a reward for this service – on top of the Outing – we now had the right to visit all the big houses, to sing our carols and collect our tribute.

To work them all in meant a five-mile foot journey over wild and generally snowed-up country. So the first thing we did was to plan our route; a formality, as the route never changed. All the same, we blew our fingers and argued; and then we chose our Leader. This was not binding, for we all fancied ourselves as Leaders, and he who started the night in that position usually trailed home with a bloody nose.

Eight of us set out that night. There was Sixpence the Tanner, who had never sung in his life (he just worked his mouth in church); the brothers Horace and Boney, who were always fighting everybody and always getting the worst of it; Clergy Green, the preaching maniac; Walt the bully, and my two brothers. As we went down the lane other boys, from other villages, were already about the hills, bawling 'Kingwenslush' and shouting through keyholes: 'Knock on the knocker! Ring at the bell! Give us a penny for singing so well!' They weren't an approved charity as we were, the Choir; but competition was in the air.

Our first call as usual was the house of the Squire, and we trouped nervously down his drive. For light we had candles in marmalade-jars suspended on loops of string, and they threw pale gleams on the towering snowdrifts that stood on each side of the drive. A blizzard was blowing, but we were well wrapped up, with Army puttees on our legs, woollen hats on our heads, and several scarves around our ears.

As we approached the Big House across its white silent lawns, we too grew respectfully silent. The lake near by was stiff and black, the waterfall frozen and still. We arranged ourselves shuffling around the big front door, then knocked and announced the Choir.

A maid bore the tidings of our arrival away into the echoing distances of the house, and while we waited we cleared our throats noisily. Then she came back, and the door was left ajar for us, and we were bidden to begin. We brought no music, the carols were in our heads. 'Let's give 'em "Wild Shepherds",' said Jack. We began in confusion, plunging into a wreckage of keys, of different words and tempo; but we gathered our strength; he who sang loudest took the rest of us with him, and the carol took shape if not sweetness.

This huge stone house, with its ivied walls, was always a mystery to us. What were those gables, those rooms and attics, those narrow windows veiled by the cedar trees? As we sang 'Wild Shepherds' we craned our necks, gaping into that lamplit hall which we had never entered; staring at the muskets and untenanted chairs, the great tapestries furred by dust – until suddenly, on the stairs, we saw the old Squire himself standing and listening with his head on one side.

He didn't move until we'd finished; then slowly he tottered towards us, dropped two coins in our box with a trembling hand, scratched his name in the book we carried, gave us each a long look with his moist blind eyes, then turned away in silence.

As though released from a spell, we took a few sedate steps, then broke into a run for the gate. We didn't stop till we were out of the grounds. Impatient, at last, to discover the extent of his bounty, we squatted by the cowsheds, held our lanterns over the book, and saw that he had written 'Two Shillings'.

This was quite a good start. No-one of any worth in the district would dare to give us less than the Squire.

So with money in the box, we pushed on up the valley, pouring scorn on each other's performance. Confident now, we began to consider our quality, and whether one carol was not better suited to us than another. Horace, Walt said, shouldn't sing at all; his voice was beginning to break. Horace disputed this and there was a brief token battle – they fought as they walked, kicking up divots of snow, then they forgot it, and Horace still sang.

Steadily we worked through the length of the valley, going from house to house, visiting the lesser and the greater gentry – the farmers, the doctors, the merchants, the majors, and other exalted persons. It was freezing hard and blowing too; yet not for a moment did we feel the cold. The snow blew into our faces, into our eyes and mouths, soaked through our puttees, got into our boots, and dripped from our woollen caps. But we did not care. The collecting-box grew heavier, and the list of names in the book longer and more extravagant, each trying to outdo the other.

Mile after mile we went, fighting against the wind, falling into snowdrifts, and navigating by the lights of the houses. And yet we never saw our audience. We called at house after house; we sang in courtyards and porches, outside windows, or in the damp gloom of hallways; we heard voices from hidden rooms; we smelt rich clothes and strange hot food; we saw maids bearing in dishes or carrying away coffee-cups; we received nuts, cakes, figs, preserved ginger, dates, cough-drops, and money; but we never once saw our patrons. We sang as it were at the castle walls, and apart from the Squire, who had shown himself to prove that he was still alive, we never expected it otherwise.

As the night drew on there was trouble with Boney. 'Noel', for instance, had a rousing harmony which Boney persisted in singing, and singing flat. The others forbade him to sing at all, and Boney said he would fight us. Picking himself up, he agreed we were right, then he disappeared altogether. He just turned away and walked into the snow and wouldn't answer when we called him back. Much later, as we reached a far point up the valley, somebody said 'Hark!' and we stopped to listen. Far away across the fields from the distant village came the sound of a frail voice singing, singing 'Noel', and singing it flat – it was Boney, branching out on his own.

We approached our last house high up on the hill, the place of Joseph the farmer. For him we had chosen a special carol, which was about the other Joseph, so that we always felt that singing it added a spicy cheek to the night. The last stretch of country to reach his farm was perhaps the most difficult of all. In these rough bare lanes, open to all winds, sheep were buried and wagons lost. Huddled together, we tramped in one another's footsteps, powdered snow blew into our screwed-up eyes, the candles burnt low, some blew out altogether, and we talked loudly above the gale.

Crossing, at last, the frozen mill-stream – whose wheel in summer still turned a barren mechanism – we climbed up to Joseph's farm. Sheltered by trees, warm on its bed of snow, it seemed always to be like this. As always it was late; as always this was our final call. The snow had a fine crust upon it, and the old trees sparkled like tinsel.

We grouped ourselves round the farmhouse porch. The sky cleared, and broad streams of stars ran down over the valley and away to Wales. On Slad's white slopes, seen through the black sticks of its woods, some red lamps still burned in the windows.

Everything was quiet; everywhere there was the faint crackling silence of the winter night. We started singing, and we were all moved by the words and the sudden trueness of our voices. Pure, very clear, and breathless we sang:

As Joseph was a walking
He heard an angel sing;
'This night shall be the birth-time
Of Christ the Heavenly King.

He neither shall be borned
In housen nor in hall,
Nor in a place of paradise
But in an ox's stall. . .'

And two thousand Christmases became real to us then; the houses, the halls, the places of paradise had all been visited; the stars were bright to guide the Kings through the snow; and across the farmyard we could hear the beasts in their stalls. We were given roast apples and hot mince-pies, in our nostrils were spices like myrrh, and in our wooden box, as we headed back for the village, there were golden gifts for all.

7

Good King Wenceslas

JIM TURNER

Jim Turner of Cirencester was born in 1903. In 1919 he became a pupil teacher at £12 a year at Sevenhampton village school, and after training college he taught in Yorkshire, Bath and several Cotswold communities before returning to his native town in 1943. When he stepped down through physical illness 20 years later he was head of Deer Park Comprehensive in Cirencester, and in his long retirement his output of poetry and verse was prolific. I have the highest regard for his reflective poems, which show great technical skill and tell of his love of his fellow man, times past and the Cotswolds in a voice very much his own. But just as apparent over the years was his ability to entertain with his keen sense of humour.

Good King Wenceslas rang Joe
Weeks before Saint Stephen's.
'What price, Joe, for Christmas snow?'
Honest Joe said: 'Evens.'
Wenceslas said: 'Watch it, please.
Now you're in my bad books.
Good my page got thirty-threes
Yesterday with La-ad-brokes.'

Snow fell thick on Christmas Day.
When he saw it dinted
Words they heard their master say
Never could be printed.
Page and monarch through the snow
Journeyed round the mountain.
What d'you know? They chucked poor Joe
In Saint Agnes' fou-oun-tain.

Under the Christmas Stars

HUMPHREY PHELPS

Strictly speaking, for a Cotswold book, Humphrey Phelps lives on the wrong side of the river on a farm near Westbury-on-Severn, but his memories of carol singing during the Second World War strike a chord with all who were country children in those confusing times.

There is a lovely evocative poem by Leonard Clark which begins: 'I had almost forgotten the singing in the streets'. After a lifetime of Decembers, he recalled carol singing in Cinderford when he was a boy:

A seasonal scene in Painswick in recent times.

'Waiting for Christmas to come,
    the boys and me
Trudging over blanket fields, waving
    Lanterns to the sky.'

Then he wondered, with the years gone, the boys and girls
scattered, if the sound of the singing in the streets was still
there. He concluded:

'And I think it may be so;
Yes, I believe it may be so.'

Five miles away and a generation later I can remember
another company of boys and girls singing carols in the lanes.
We had no waving lanterns because these were the dark days of

war. There were also no warm, welcoming glows from windows or doorways, and even car lights were confined to the minimum.

In memory, at least, the stars were always shining brightly on Christmas Eve, lighting our way as an earlier and brighter star had guided those upon the first Christmas. Yes, I remember our singing in the lanes, the boys and girls who are now grandparents. Unlike Clark's companions, they have not scattered; most of them still live in the district.

I remember the keen air which reddened our faces and brought a glow to our cheeks, the tang of frost, grass verges of the lanes crisp and white. The darkened houses with darkened doorways as they opened, and the welcome from within, the mugs of sharp cider at the farmhouses. The farmers were generous with this, and with the boys it was a matter of honour to drink as much of it as was offered. Any other form of alcohol would have been strictly forbidden, but cider, for some reason, was regarded as innocuous, even by those whose experience should have taught them otherwise.

If the sound of our singing in the lanes is still there, I can only hope it has improved with the passing years. The girls sang well enough, but the boys were indifferent at best, raucous at worst, as the night progressed. We did, however, pride ourselves on our spirited rendering of *Good King Wenceslas* – how we bellowed 'Bring me flesh and bring me wine' and stretched 'Croo-oo-el' to a length that was itself cruel.

We would have sung Wenceslas at every house and drowned the more melodious voices, but the girls wisely insisted upon singing other carols as well. They not only sang better, they behaved better, taking to walking ahead of us while we dawdled and sang secular songs between the often distant houses, the line of *Show Me The Way To Go Home* that went 'I had a little drink about an hour ago' proclaiming the obvious.

As we approached the next house the girls nagged and scolded, and to some measure succeeded in inducing some decorum to our behaviour. And by arriving at the door ahead of us, they were able to launch into the carol of their choice, thus saving the inhabitants from our boisterous Wenceslas. On second thought, I think the sounds of our singing that carol may still be there in the lanes.

Christmas 1945 was probably our last time. That year our company was augmented by one who had spent the previous Christmas in a prison camp in Germany, and this was the first true season of peace after six years of war. The stars shone above and lights blazed from windows, doorways and human hearts. We were young, the world was old and tired after those long years of fighting, but it seemed young to us.

Hark! The Herald Angels Sing; there was cause for us to sing with the angels, for Peace on Earth was a reality rather than a longed-for wish. But that was also the first Christmas that the bright star of Bethlehem was shadowed by a dark, mushroom-shaped cloud. Then, we in our youth, and those older and wiser than ourselves, did not comprehend the evil enormity of that cloud which still casts its shadow. Yet children still sing in the streets and lanes at Christmas – so perhaps, before it is too late, the rulers of the world will listen to them and grasp the message heralded by the bright star of the first Christmas.

from

Cotswold Days

COLIN HOWARD

Cotswold Days, first published in 1937, is largely unknown to the present generation of readers. It is very much a book of its time and cannot claim any great literary style, but those who remember Gloucester in the years before the last war see its description of the city's Christmas bustle of 1936 as a true and touching evocation of those times.

It seems that it will be Christmas at any moment. The Christmas Market was held last Monday, that stormy day after the snow. It was certainly the wildest Christmas Market Day within living memory.

The Christmas Market, of course, is a very special one, when the finest cattle come under the hammer, and although I did not see these cattle myself this year, their huge carcases will soon be displayed in the butchers' shops in all their gargantuan might, adorned rather pathetically with the rosettes their bulk won for them in a life whose only destiny was death.

Gloucester makes ready for Christmas far more heartily than Cheltenham. But then, Gloucester works for its living and is proud of it, and Cheltenham does not talk much about money, but genteelly assumes you have it.

In Gloucester the streets rumble with carts stacked preca-

'Gloucester works for its living and is proud of it': Northgate
Street in the 1920s.

riously high with holly and mistletoe, and if there is a more
seasonable sight, I should like to know what it is. Gloucestershire is one of those few favoured shires in which
mistletoe grows, but it does the thing handsomely, and grows
with rich profusion. So many cart loads of greenery are there
that you can picture the festive appearances the rooms in all
the Gloucester houses will be wearing in a few days. You know
just how it would look if you took the lid off Gloucester.

When I first came here, I thought that Greenhill Cottage
would not be gregarious enough to attract carol singers, but no
such thing. However, country carol singers are infinitely
preferable to their town brethren, who stop unashamedly short
in the middle of unimpassioned delivery of a line, grab the
largesse offered them, mutter a perfunctory 'Thank-y'-merry-
Christmas', and scuttle next door, avid to make the most of

the racket while the season lasts. In the country you feel that the carollers do recognise that it is a hymn that they are singing, and they do not go when you have given them money, but stay to sing another carol or two.

The earliest carol singers I ever heard were many years ago – I think it was in 1921 – when a little girl and a considerably more little boy solemnly sang *While Shepherds Watched Their Flocks By Night* on November the Fifth. We were engaged with

'Cheltenham does not talk much about money, but genteelly assumes you have it': a beautifully atmospheric study of The Promenade, *c.* 1950, by Hugo van Wadenoyen.

a bonfire at the bottom of the garden, in signalisation of the anniversary more usually connected with that date. In view of their diminutive stature, the singers were probably wise to get in early, before more robust competition elbowed them aside. Nevertheless, carol singing is not a whole-time occupation that should be relied on to bring in a steady income all the year round, and this Bertie explained to them, softening matters with twopence.

The girl, the spokesman of the party – her brother was too young to talk, and could only sing; possibly he couldn't even do that, and was only present by way of moral support – said they were practising for Christmas. Evidently she considered dress rehearsals worth charging admission to. Or maybe we represented the provincial tour for polishing up prior to West End production. Anyhow, with so much time for practising, they must have been pretty good by Christmas.

On the hills, the Chalford Brass Band always visited us on Christmas Eve. I can see them now, just outside the door, grouped about a lantern slung from a pole, and playing as softly as their brass would allow. And there were Mummers from Bisley. They performed a local variation of the traditional Mummers' Play. I wish I could recollect that more distinctly. They came into the hall for it, the four of them – Saint George, the Captain, the Turk and the Doctor.

Every character introduced himself on his appearance, thus: 'In comes I, bold Saint George,' 'Then in comes I, the noble Captain,' and so on. The Turk got the worse of the duel, which was fought with much circumspection because of the glass inner-doors to our hall, but the Doctor, who supplied the comic relief, fortunately arrived on the scene; having given a recital of the ills he cured he turned his attention to the stricken man, with the happiest results.

Saint George, I remember, was the Bisley blacksmith. I do not know who the other three were. None of them knew where the play came from. It had survived from mouth to mouth. I doubt if it had ever been committed to paper.

At Cooper's Hill, where we spent one Christmas, there were so few children that what there were had a corner in carol singing. The drawback to this was that they could not pay return dates without being detected, and evoking the suspicious: 'You've been here before, haven't you?'

But the memory of this kind that gives me the greatest pleasure is of the band at Painswick, where we spent our first Christmas after leaving Bussage. They went round the streets very early on Christmas morning, and awakened me by playing just outside my window. It was rather thrilling to listen to them. It was perfectly dark, and when I looked at my watch I saw that the time was just four o' clock. They played three carols, and I hoped very much they would play more, but the next sound was the soft tramp of feet, and when they played again it was distant.

Old Corder was trying to sell me a bunch of mistletoe in the pub last night.

''Tes just what thee wants for thicky cottage o' thine,' he told me.

I didn't ask him what he meant by that.

'Right good mistletoe, this yere be,' he continued, holding it up and shaking it enticingly before me. 'Never failed yet, I do assure 'ee.'

'Why, has it been up somewhere already?' I asked.

He grinned.

'No, but every bit o' mistletoe do grow on a tree, don' 'um? And I do know the archard this yere bit come from.'

'I'm surprised at you, Mr. Corder!' said Mrs. Early. 'Fancy you knowing it, at your age!'

He grinned the wider, with the vanity of old age accused even in levity of amorous exploits.

'In comes I, bold St. George . . .': Bisley mummers *c.* 1940.

'That archard 'a' seed a sight o' fun,' he said. ''Tes a wonder the trees did bear a single apple this year, the way them young things did shake the blossom off.'

The pub was looking very attractive last night, with a great fire rivalling the oil lamp with its flickering flames, and holly stuck everywhere it would go, and gay paper chains festooning the ceiling. There was Christmas in the air. The very beer seemed to taste more festive.

'Why don't you *give* the gennelman your mistletoe?' suggested Harry Woodman. '*Thee* don't need no mistletoe! Thee can do purty well wi'out it, I know!'

'Aye, that I can, you!' answered old Corder complacently. 'A' right, sir, I'll give 'ee the mistletoe, and I do 'ope as it'll give thee a right 'appy Christmas.'

18

So, of course, I bought it from him, which gave rise to more jocularities, especially when I observed (meaning, of course, that I had nowhere to hang it) that I shouldn't know what to do with it.

Yes, everything in Gloucester is conducive to the Christmas spirit. England is well on the way to winning the second Test Match in Australia, thanks almost entirely to Hammond, who has made 231 not out, whilst Barnett, who opened for England, is the next highest scorer with 57. We expected our representatives to do well, but this in no way mitigates against our delight at their success.

True, Newport beat Gloucester at rugby football, and beat us rather badly. 'But,' as everybody has remarked many times, 'look at our backs – only Parker and Hook of the regulars.'

Tonight I have been doing the last of my Christmas shopping, in company with what appears to be most of the county. However, it is the time of the year when crowded shops do not cause resentment, but rather add to the spirit of things. Every shop blazes with light, somehow succeeding in looking like a ship in full sail. The fishmongers are unrecognisable behind their great masks of turkeys hanging in curtains from above the upper windows. Inside, there are turkeys and more turkeys and yet more turkeys – turkeys hanging from nails, turkeys on the marble slabs, turkeys lying unplucked in heaps on the floors, turkeys being brought in constantly from the backs. It is all turkey. Fish just doesn't get a look-in.

At the stationers', the tables of Christmas cards are densely hemmed with people, some picking at random, others going for the picture, and others again being guided by the poetic sentiments within. Sometimes the verse leads to the jettisoning of an attractive picture; sometimes the picture wins, despite the unsuitably lurid warmth of the affectionate wording. Robins, stagecoaches waiting outside inns, churches in snowstorms with appropriate sprigs of holly, cats drowsily warming themselves before fires – all the seasonable features honoured by time are there, together with a great many whose appositeness is not at first apparent, such as crinolined ladies watering gardens improbably floriferous, subtle sprays of forget-me-nots and inviting seashores.

The Covered Market in Eastgate is thronged. 'The earth is the Lord's, and the fullness thereof,' says the inscription over the portals, and 'fullness' just about hits the nail on the head tonight. The stalls, that seem always about to avalanche the unwontedly piled merchandise to the floor, are beset with purchasers all unreasonably and clamorously desirous of being served next, so that it would be a miracle of memory that the assistants give the purchase and the change to the same person, were it not for the hand extended in quiet insistence.

Down Westgate Street a steady flow turns into Woolworth's, where a current of humanity against which it is both useless and needless to fight carries you in a comprehensive tour of the counters. The press of men and women is so great that it seems incredible that there should also exist a considerable substratum of children, in proof of which you have only to glance down and observe that there are two or three packed, heaven knows how, around your own legs.

The library at Boots's, where I go to exchange a book, demonstrates by its emptiness that this is no time for such idle work as reading. But the body of the shop has no such atmosphere of leisure. Here, again, the absorbing pastime of Christmas card selection is being pursued with great earnestness and a singleness of purpose that is insensible to the children who tug at the theoretically attendant elders, in mute reminder that they are still there. At one counter I see a much benephewed and benieced friend loading himself steadily with children's annuals. At another a young man is evidently solving the entire present question with a purchase of scent of a

E. Broadhurst's shop, York Buildings, Bath, *c.* 1910.

magnitude that would almost justify his claiming a discount. At a third counter another friend is preparing for some abstruse Yuletide devilry by buying greasepaint 'to make me look like an arab', so he mysteriously stipulates.

Most people I know in Gloucester seem to be abroad tonight, but none has enough freedom of time or of arms for more than an expansive smile or greeting. Sybil wanders by, lips moving; either she has lost her shopping list and is trying to recall the items thereon, or she relies entirely on memory. I ask her which it is.

21

'There!' she exclaims, annoyed. 'Now you've made me forget!'

Fred swoops past me on his motorcycle, leaving me to marvel that any man occupied with the riding of his machine and the guarding of a redundancy of brown paper packages can yet spare a hand to wave. The twins stare so earnestly into a shop window that they see my reflection behind them, and, turning round with such impetuousness as to shed one or two outlying parcels, inquire with twinly unison whether I can think of anything that would appeal to Bill. Mary goes over the Cross in her car, a bag of golf sticks standing on the seat at her side. Heavens! Do people really play golf when the great game of Christmas shopping is on hand?

To my surprise I discover that my own arms have accumulated an aggregation of parcels. I seek my car, parked in the quiet dimness of Market Parade, and once there, am disinclined to leave it.

So I start up the engine and drive home, up into the fresh, cool hills, leaving the distant glitter of Gloucester, concealing its seasonal turmoil, behind me.

And so the year goes out, and that is the end of 1936, or very nearly. Another year gone, imperceptibly, day by day, making one think in its passing that it will always be spring, always be summer, always be autumn – and then, Christmas, and the realisation that the last few days must be clung to and savoured feverishly or they, too, will be gone in the tail of their kin.

Robin Redbreast

LEONARD CLARK

You are a strange bird,
a little bundle of contradictions.

If I come near where you peck for food
near the house in the frosted garden,
you do not flit away into the bushes,
you welcome me with song,
you are my friend;
let another bird invade your territory,
you drive him away in anger.

You make your bulky nest in winter,
weaving it beautifully, grasses, wool and moss,
choosing sometimes a hole in a wall,
but as often an old kettle, end of a drain,
even setting up house in church,
lay five or six speckled eggs;
other birds wait for the spring.

And for your pocket size,
what a loud singer you are,
sharp, clear notes
cutting the silences when late afternoon
dims into misted twilight.

Of all birds, the most eccentric.

from

The Season of the Year

JOHN MOORE

Moore (1907–67) was living in Bredon when this collection of his rural reflections was published in 1954; the newspaper of Christmas, 1877 refers to events in his home town of Tewkesbury.

Christmas, of course, is never what it was. We are reminded of this fact every year by old Jeremy Skinner, whose memory goes back seventy years or so and who sadly shakes his head as the landlord brings in the holly-sprigs to decorate his bar. 'In the old days,' says Jeremy, 'there was *real berries* on the holly, not just a little pip here and there. You could scarce see the leaves for red berries. That was because winters were harder then. Nature provided the berries as food for the birds.'

Always on Christmas Eve he pulls out of his pocket, and passes round the company in the bar, a very faded yellowing photograph in which he takes pleasure and pride. It represents a butcher's shop in the nearby town, and bears on its back the inscription 'Christmas 1913'. If you look carefully – and Jeremy will insist that you do – you will make out, as it were through the mists of time, an array of enormous sides of beef, a dozen at least hanging from their hooks, with innumerable legs of mutton and loins of pork. Among them stands the proud butcher in his striped apron; at least Jeremy assures you it is the butcher, though his huge hands are like lumps of beef and his broad features peering between the haunches are liable to be confused with a boar's head.

'Look at it,' says Jeremy grimly. 'Just look. I simply ask you to look, that's all.'

We look.

'The rosettes,' says Jeremy, '– You can just see 'em, up there in the left-hand corner – were worn by the prize-winning beasts at the Christmas Fat Stock Fair. Never bought anything but the best, he didn't. His sirloins would melt in your mouth. When I looked at my Christmas joint – if you call it a joint – this evening, and when I thought of those sirloins, well . . . believe it or not, but I minds the time when my old mother, and she was a hale and hearty woman, *couldn't lift down* our Christmas joint out of the larder; and "Jeremy," she called, "Jeremy me boy, just come here and give us a hand. . ."'

You would think, to listen to Jeremy, that Father Christmas had become a tattered beggar dressed in rags, that he who was once fat and prosperous and prodigal was now a pale starveling waif. And perhaps there would be some truth in this sad picture if the festival were simply a matter of beef and booze; instead of being a mood, a spirit, a leaven, something imponderable, a high wind blowing through our hearts. It is much more profound a mystery, fortunately, than the sirloins and the fat butcher in Jeremy's photograph; although even they are becoming a trifle mysterious as our memories fade and the photograph fades and the too too solid flesh melts into a peasoup fog.

'– There,' says Jeremy, pointing at the bottom left-hand corner with an old gnarled finger, 'that was snow.'

And indeed the photograph is flecked all over with white spots which we had thought were due to its great age.

'Snow,' repeats Jeremy firmly. 'When that photo was took, it was snowing. And it went on snowing for a week. None of your new-fangled green Christmases then! It snowed for a week and, on Christmas Day, after church, we sat in here at noon drinking our beer by candlelight. Why by candlelight? Because the drifts was above the winders of the bar, see. Drink our beer by candlelight we did, and when I say beer I mean beer, not this belly-chilling stuff we get today. . . .'

But last year, as a kind of corrective to Jeremy's seasonal recollections, I took the trouble to dip into the files of our small local newspaper; and in the leading article for Christmas 1877 I was amused to find, almost word for word, the very complaint about the weather which Jeremy makes in the pub every year:

'The so-called old-fashioned Christmas is becoming so much a thing of the past as only to be talked of by the old folks, and even the hoary-headed and icicle-bearded old Father seems gradually to be losing his identity as a seasonable association.'

It goes on to mention *'weather of spring-like geniality'*, and *'The Xmas dinner partaken of with the sun streaming through the window with the brilliancy of May.'*

So much for Jeremy's six-foot snowdrifts and six-week frosts!

When I had read the leading article I looked through the advertisements. Most of them adopted the exclamatory style which was then in fashion: OVERCOATS! OVERCOATS!! or LAMPS! LAMPS!! LAMPS!!! or BICYCLES!!! BICYCLES!!!! (innovations which certainly deserved four exclamation marks in 1877). The workhouse asked for tenders for the supply of port, brandy, gin, whisky and beer, which suggests that in one respect at least the Victorian Poor Law was more humane than our present-day substitute. The wines and spirits cost about two shillings a bottle, and the most expensive drink in the advertisement columns was not champagne (2s 2d) but Holland's (2s 8d).

Seasonal entertainment, at the Philharmonic Hall, was strangely varied in 1877. You could choose between a troupe of Japanese gymnasts, some negro minstrels and a lecture on the Devils and Demons of the Scriptures. Organised sport seemed to be confined to a sparrow shoot – 'For Prizes: Fat Geese' – and a football match which, hazarded the editor darkly, 'will no doubt be full of interesting incidents.' This prediction proved accurate: the next week's issue contained a public notice: 'CAUTION TO FOOTBALL PLAYERS. In consequence of the damage which has been done to Mitton Leys by persons playing football there, notice is hereby given that any further play after the date of this notice is forbidden.'

There is a charming Christmas greeting to his patrons from Mr. Hadley, the London Hair Cutter, 'whose present practice averages nearly 400 Hair Cuttings per month.' 'Do not,' he begs them, 'yield to the rash act of shaving the head, which in 99 cases out of 100 may be dispensed with and a good Head of Hair preserved to old age.' In an adjoining paragraph a Mr. Craddock publicly expresses his regret for trespassing in pursuit of game on the land of Mr. Bishop and 'consents to pay the cost of the advertisement in consideration of his abstaining from taking proceedings' – a curious form of expiation.

But perhaps the most remarkable advertisement of all is one issued by the newspaper itself, which had fallen on lean times, and sought to revive its flagging circulation with a free gift scheme very like those adopted by national newspapers in the 1930s. The gift (in return for a year's subscription to the journal) consisted of a coloured oleograph entitled *The Gypsy Queen;* and the editor almost forgot that he was a highly respectable Victorian when he sat down to describe the beauties of this work of art. 'Upon the marble terrace of a

Neapolitan palace is *The Gypsy Queen*. She has just cast off her sandals, and with bare feet she commences one of those wild and yet graceful dances so peculiar to her race. With her well-rounded arms held aloft she spins about; and her rapid gyrations, expressing perfectly what has been so well styled the "poetry of motion", have cast loose the silken strings that bind the bodice of her picturesque costume and revealed her well-rounded form.' ('Well-rounded' seems to have been the editor's favourite expression; I think he felt it was as far as he dared go). 'Coal-black is her eye, raven her hair,' he continues, 'against the beautiful background of the famous Bay of Naples! And behind her the volcano Vesuvius stands ready to burst out at a moment's notice and carry desolation into the fair country around!'

So much for the Editor's Christmas Gift To His Readers. Let us return to the Seasonable Festivities. There was, of

'The drifts was above the winders of the bar, see . . .': the road out of Bisley, March 1916.

28

course, the annual Fat Stock Show, and although it was a time of agricultural depression — according to Trevelyan the whole structure of English agriculture had 'collapsed' in 1875 — the total turnover at the Christmas market exceeded £7,000. In the same market town this year it will probably be less than £1,000. Top prices were £42 for a fat heifer, 86s for a sheep and £8 14s for a bacon pig. Christmas was the heyday of the butchers, and nearly a dozen served the small town of 4,000 inhabitants. Each held an exhibition of huge sides and haunches and choice cuts; and the editor sent his reporter around from shop to shop to describe the display. Unfortunately, this reporter seems to have been a queasy fellow, and the spectacle of so much raw flesh proved almost too much for him. He expressed his gratification that 'to some extent this year the immense mounds of nausea-provoking yellow fat have given way to an equal distribution of fat and lean,' but observed in a subsequent paragraph that 'A superfluity of solid fat is evidently the standard of perfection at this season, and so in common with the rest we admire it, but not from any beauty which so questionable a virtue confers on it to our own taste.'

The Mayor, of course, gave a Municipal Banquet, and the paper printed his menu on the front page: a good square meal without airs and graces or fancy faldadiddles, enough to make any man sleep all afternoon in his chair:

Mock-turtle or Oxtail Soup
Turbot with Lobster Sauce or Cod with Oyster Sauce or Eels *a la Tartare*
Savoury Rissoles or Oyster Patties
Roast Turkey, Sirloin, Haunch of Mutton, Chicken or Tongue
Roast Venison, Pheasant or Hare
Plum Pudding, Cheese Cakes
Dessert

Having, as our fastidious reporter puts it, partaken, the
company proceeded to drink no fewer than 14 toasts, to the
Queen, to Parliament, to the Army, to the Navy, to the
Bishops, Clergy and all the Christian Ministers, to the Ladies,
to the Visitors, to every conceivable local dignitary, and finally
to the Prosperity of the Town.

The Christmas number from which I have taken these
extracts was published on December 23rd; so I turned to the
issue of December 30th to learn how the various festivities
turned out. The leading article congratulates all concerned
that the season of goodwill had passed off 'peacefully' – as if
dark doings had been expected and feared. But it adds a
curious proviso – *'Except for the desperado who presented himself at
the Bell Hotel on Christmas Eve.'* Nowhere else in the paper can I
find mention of this desperado; so he passes into oblivion, and
since he never appeared in the police court we must assume
that he escaped into the dark from whence he came.

It is curious, that sigh of relief in the leading article that
nothing untoward had occurred, and one hears it again in the
account of Christmas Day at the workhouse: 'The children
looked happy and healthy, and though expressing their
enjoyment in various ways were nevertheless well conducted.'
There is a distinct suggestion that the children were dangerous
animals who might at any moment turn and bite the hand
which fed them; and one feels that the Mayor or Vicar who cut
the Christmas cake had a sense of perilous adventure as he did
so, as if he had ventured into a lions' den.

The sparrow-shoot, one is glad to learn, also passed off 'in a
remarkably orderly manner' – as if this was not always the
case. Three sparrows were released from the trap for each of the
competitors; and the shooting wasn't very good, for the winner
of the Fat Goose managed to bag only two of them. The report
explains apologetically: 'Anyone versed in this matter is aware
what a difficult little chap the sparrow is to hit.' When the

shoot was over the competitors partook of a curious repast consisting of cherry brandy, plum pudding and cheese.

The police court held on the day after Boxing Day sprouted its usual crop of holiday miscreants – 'drunk and disorderly' was apparently so familiar a charge that the paper shortens it to D.D. The Royal Navy in its payrolls uses the same abbreviation to express a casualty: Discharged Dead; and this was indeed the fate of one of the drunkards, for we read of the Lamentable Death from Drink of one Elizabeth Hodges. This was the only serious casualty, although a Mr. Jellyman assaulted his neighbour who 'in the course of conversation called his wife a liar', and a Mr. Harris beat with a thick stick some carol singers who took the liberty of breaking his door down when he failed to answer the bell. A farmer was fined for failing to report a case of sheep scab to the police. This was the last case, and the chairman took the opportunity of congratulating the town on a peaceful and well-conducted holiday season. 'Some ill-sorted scoundrel,' he was bound to admit, had painted the Mayor's house blue on Christmas Eve, and so far he had not been apprehended; but this, one feels, was regarded by all as a mere peccadillo, a slightly too boisterous frolic not altogether out of accord with the Christmas spirit. The Justices rose.

But there still remains, to tease and tickle our fancy, the unsolved mystery of the desperado who presented himself at the Bell. What it was that he did there is forever hidden from us. We shall never know who he was or how he escaped the just retribution which was meted out to the D.D.s and to Mr. Jellyman and to the misanthropic Mr. Harris, who had no appreciation of a seasonal song. He slips away into the limbo of history, a sinister and shadowy figure who stepped out of the night into the bright and holly-draped bar, performed his anonymous and desperate deed, and vanished into the murky darkness.

B.C.: A.D.

U. A. FANTHORPE

Ursula Fanthorpe of Wotton-under-Edge is ranked highly
among contemporary British poets, a status consolidated by
her success in several major competitions and the publica-
tion of a selection of her works by Penguin in 1986. Cool
understatement characterises much of her work, disguising
a style that is rich in imagery and inventive thought and
direct in its emotional appeal.

This was the moment when Before
Turned into After, and the future's
Uninvented timekeepers presented arms.

This was the moment when nothing
Happened. Only dull peace
Sprawled boringly over the earth.

This was the moment when even energetic Romans
Could find nothing better to do
Than counting heads in remote provinces.

And this was the moment
When a few farm workers and three
Members of an obscure Persian sect

Walked haphazard by starlight straight
Into the kingdom of heaven.

32

Going A-Thomasing

HYLDA KING-ROSS

Within living memory the custom of going a-Thomasing, also known as gooding or mumping, was widespread on St. Thomas's Day, 21 December. It was a kind of begging dignified by tradition, in which members of poorer families would call on better-off neighbours – the squire in particular, in estate villages – for gifts of food or money. In 1972 Hylda King-Ross, whose family lived at Beckford Hall, near Tewkesbury, until 1935, recalled the scene at her home on the morning of December 21.

All the workers on our estate sent their wives or mothers, with the small children, round to our house. The women wore fascinating large white bonnets, shawls over their shoulders and long skirts down to the ground, from behind which some of the very young children would peep shyly.

When the weather was very cold and snowy we youngsters used to watch from an upstairs window as the procession formed up in a semi-circle round the front door steps. We would call out to each other 'Here they come' with great excitement as more and more came in sight up the drive.

At length all had arrived, generally forty or so, young and old, tall and short, and one of them would walk up to the steps and give the bell a good pull. We always listened for this, and as we heard the ring echoing in the old stone passages below, we knew the pantry door would open and the butler would walk solemnly to answer the bell. Then he returned to summon my father to the scene.

In the meantime there was a stir in the little waiting crowd; feet began to shuffle, whispers were exchanged about the cold morning, hands were rubbed violently – more with nervous excitement than with cold, very often – and then all heads were turned as the big old oak-studded door opened slowly, and out came my father.

He carried a leather bag, and gave a sixpenny piece to each person to help to buy Christmas fare. In those days sixpence was worth much more than it is today. He would say a few words of greeting and cheer to each woman, and they in turn would shake his hand and say with a smile and a bob curtsey: 'Thank you, sir, and a very happy Christmas to you, I'm sure, and to the family.'

The little ceremony over, they would all walk round to the back door, lining both sides of the approach, the halt and lame bringing up the rear.

Then they were each given a steaming hot cup of coffee, and plenty of bread spread thickly with lovely farm butter. Sometimes a couple of slices were pushed into an already bulging pocket. It was a simple but touching picture, and brought the spirit of Christmas into the air.

This old custom had been in existence in Gloucestershire for a very long time, I was told, and had been carried out at our house from Elizabethan days.

from

Portrait of Elmbury

JOHN MOORE

This novel was the first of John Moore's Brensham Trilogy, which made a firm impression on the British literary scene of the late 1940s, remains in print to this day and inspired a successful television series in the early 1980s. Elmbury, of course, is the author's home town of Tewkesbury, where he first started work in the family auctioneers' business.

There was one day that fell in early December more exciting than Christmas itself; the day of Christmas market. Always on this occasion my father's firm provided sandwiches and drinks for all comers: dealers, smallholders, cowmen, shepherds, drovers. The more substantial farmers were entertained to luncheon at the Swan. Great were the preparations on the day before the market. Enormous joints sizzled in Old Cookie's oven; baskets of loaves lay everywhere about the kitchen, huge pats of yellow butter, tongues, sausages, pasties. Maids were busy all day cutting sandwiches, which were piled on dishes and covered with napkins. There was an air of bustle and festivity all over the house; but alas, the festive spirit coupled with the near approach of Christmas was too much for Old Cookie; when the last joint was roasted, she got drunk.

35

Portrait of Elmbury: Tewkesbury looking down Church Street
from The Cross at the end of the First World War.

Lachrymose, incoherent, completely plastered, she confronted
my mother and was given the sack. Next morning, sick and
repentant, she was re-engaged.

Although the sale did not begin until half past eleven, the
first beasts began to pass our window as early as half past nine.
Thenceforward for two hours there passed down Elmbury
High Street a procession such as might serve as a country
counterpart of a Lord Mayor's Show. But here were no city
financiers whose riches were scraps of paper locked in safes –
riches which might disappear tomorrow if somebody else
juggled with his shares more cunningly.

Here was solid wealth, the real wealth of England, a sight
that would have warmed old Cobbett's heart to see: fat oxen,
sleek and ponderous, white-faced Herefords curly-haired

between their straight horns, Shorthorns as rich red as the fresh-turned loam, dark as the winter ploughland where the sweat stained their sides; flocks of sheep, broad and flat-backed so that the collies could run about on top of them, thick-woolled, black-faced Oxfords, whose multitudinous breaths in the frosty air made a mist which moved as their great flocks moved like rivers down the street; and huge fat waddling pigs, sows whose bellies had brought forth great litters and which now brushed the earth between their short legs, bacons, porkers, Large Whites, Large Blacks, Middle Whites, blue-mottled crossbreds, sandy Tamworths and the ancient dappled breed of Gloster Spots.

Here was the annual harvest of the great stock-fattening farms which lay in the rich valleys of the two rivers; here was a season's consummation, the happy outcome of the marriage between English weather and English soil, delivered by the skill and patience of men whose grandfathers had owned their farms before them.

To this end the turgid waters of last winter's floods had left their rich alluvial deposit in the meadows, so that the spring grass sprung more greenly; to this end in Elmbury Ham in June, and in a thousand such great hayfields, sweaty men with pitchforks had built a village of sweet-smelling ricks; to this end swedes and turnips and mangel-wurzels, plump roots nearly as big as a football, had alternated in their proper rotations with golden corn and brown fallow on the slopes of the gentle hills which rose from the valleys. And now the purpose of all these labours was manifest. Down the street towards the market on slow hoofs waddled the Champion Beast, great-shouldered, broad-sided, deep-flanked; and a hundred more that were nearly his match. No man so poor that he could not taste a steak on Sunday; no family in such straits that they would not see a joint on their table on Christmas Day.

Just as the Lord Mayor's Show provides its moments of comic relief, so did this splendid progress towards the Christmas market. The calf that planted its legs four-square and flatly refused to budge, though one man heaved at its halter and another pulled its tail; the fat goodwife with a couple of cackling geese under her arms; the bull which entered Double Alley and rampaged about there, so that even the Hooks made common cause against it: all these events were matters for mirth and jesting.

And later in the day, when the market was over and the farmers with bulging pockets rollicked home – when the drovers rich with Christmas tips began their Christmas pub crawl – when the butcher who had bought the Champion

'The first beasts began to pass our windows as early as half past nine . . .': the cattle market in High Street and The Plain, Thornbury in 1908.

38

Beast paraded him through the town with rosettes on his horns, a mighty fat butcher with a mighty fat beast – what merry greetings passed, what practical joking went on!

I shall never forget the butcher's face wreathed in smiles when he met Mr. Jeffs, who had bred and fattened the champion; beaming at each other, they shook hands, and the crowd in the street cheered and shouted. I shall never forget the butcher's obvious pride that he had paid the highest price for the best animal. Nowadays, it seems to me, too many people take pride in having bought something cheap; but the butcher was proud because he had bought something good, and had paid well for it.

And so dusk fell, and the lamplighter went round with his long pole, the gas lamps glowed yellow, even that wan, cloudy nebulus that burned at the entrance to Double Alley, and the last of the country people went home. Only a few belated drovers still hung about the pubs; and the first carol singers gathered round our front door to tell their old tale of peace on earth and goodwill among men.

Kiltie, The Christmas Gift Horse

DIANA ALEXANDER

Diana Alexander of Syde, near Cirencester, is a prolific writer for magazines in Gloucestershire and beyond. This true story happened in 1980, and many people in Pony Club circles in the Cotswolds will have the fondest memories of its hero.

As dusk crept over the fields that mid-December afternoon I knew I had to take action. I had reassured myself that my ponies – for once – were safely enclosed, but the constant ringing of the phone made it clear that something four-footed was loose in the village.

I trudged into the gloom with my ten-year-old daughter until we came face-to-face with a bewildered looking pony in the middle of a narrow lane. When Emily stepped forward to catch him he seemed positively relieved, and he took to our field as if it were Heaven.

I spent the evening on the telephone trying to trace his owners. I had no luck, but news travels fast, and next morning they were in touch, thanking me profusely and wondering whether I would like to borrow him for a while. I refused politely, explaining that I was already overstocked; at the same time, I could not help recalling that as a child I had longed for a pony for Christmas more than anything else in the world.

Refusal or no, no-one came to collect him, and on Christmas morning he was there to wolf down the extra goodies we sentimentally give our animals then. At around the time of the Queen's speech his owners came to wish him the compliments of the season in their Rolls Royce. But still nothing was said about his return, and for the rest of the winter he made himself at home in our windswept field.

The harsh weather gave way to spring and Rachel, a neighbour who helped me with the horses, took to riding him. She was instantly impressed. 'He's a super jumper, Di,' she told me.

That proved to be the understatement of the year. Inquiries revealed that Kiltie had jumped – and won – for many a season throughout Britain and on the Continent. As a five-year-old he had won a first prize at Hickstead for the animal with the best jumping style – and here we were, winners of a few small prizes at very local shows, with this doughty champion.

What was oddest of all was how our at first unwanted Christmas present took to his new home. Having previously been a Houdini of the highest order he never again tried to escape, and even gave the impression of enjoying the miles he hacked with me.

After his years in the big time, how quickly he settled into the rough-and-tumble of two-tent gymkhanas on sloping Cotswold meadows, Pony Club camps and gentle jaunts around Misarden Park. My elder daughter Kate jumped him, too, tentatively at first, and then with increasing confidence and success. Wherever we took him he was recognised, and we were envied. Often ambitious mothers would ask me to name my price. A price? For Kiltie? For the Christmas gift I had shunned, and with whom we would now never part? My tactic was simply to tell them that he wasn't mine to sell – and besides, he was almost twenty years old.

The years sat so lightly on his broad shoulders that we would never have believed his age if others had not kept remarking on it. 'Good heavens, is that pony *still* alive?' one doyenne of the county's horsey world would exclaim every time she saw him, though the question was purely rhetorical. In his last year he was still in the ribbons, usually competing against ponies a quarter of his age.

As he was the greediest of a piggish group, Christmas was always Kiltie's favourite time of year. Once it almost caused a disaster. For a treat I had let him loose in the garden, where there was more grass than in his field. As the day was mild I had also left the front door open, and it was only the thud of iron-clad feet on the parquet floor that alerted me to the sight of him bearing down on the Christmas tree, his teeth gnashing hopefully.

He gave us so much pleasure, so much of himself, so many laughs, that we began to think him indestructible; it still seems impossible to believe that he will never again beat all the rest to the gate on Christmas morning for his extra apples, carrots and Polo mints.

His end, one sunny autumn morning, was as swift and dignified as he deserved. Only the day before he had been jumping across country with his usual exuberance, his nostrils flaring in the brisk Cotswold air he loved. By our reckoning he was in his twenty-seventh year.

We shall never forget Kiltie, and we know there will never be another pony like him. But still at this time of year, when the lights are going on in the late afternoon, I think of those fateful phone calls half my children's lifetime ago, and my reluctance to accept that Christmas present of purest gold.

Gloucester's Domesday Christmas, 1085

That unique record of England in Norman times, the Domesday Book, dates from twenty years after the Conquest, 1086. It was a massive undertaking. The book listed 363 settlements in Gloucestershire alone, and four commissioners visited the county to hold inquiries in Gloucester, Cirencester, Winchcombe, Bristol and the Forest of Dean. But what makes it all the more remarkable is the fact that plans for it were laid down only during the previous Christmas of 1085, when William the Conqueror was with his court in Gloucester.

It was apparently his practice to spend the depths of the winter in the city. One tradition has it that he and his ministers met in the chapter house of the cathedral, but that would have borne no resemblance to today's building of that name. There is also a record of their meeting in a 'long work room'; from what we know of the way in which the Normans worked, this could have been a large temporary hut used by masons employed on a major building project.

What we know of William's visit that Christmas comes from the Anglo-Saxon Chronicle, which said: 'At mid-winter the king was at Gloucester with his witan, and there held his court five days; and afterwards the archbishop and clergy had a synod of three days . . . After this the king had very deep speech with the witan about this land, how it was peopled, and by

Stephen Reid's interpretation of William I's ordering of the compilation of the Domesday Book, Christmas 1085. This picture, displaying more artistic licence than historical accuracy, was presented to Gloucester Corporation in 1922.

what men. Then he sent his men all over England . . . what or how much each man had . . . in land or in cattle, and how much money he might be worth; so very narrowly he caused it to be traced out that there was not one single hide nor yard of land, nor even – it is a shame to tell, though it seemed to him no shame to do – an ox, nor a cow, nor a swine was left that was not set down in the writ.'

William felt secure in Gloucester, and he counted the Forest of Dean as a favourite hunting ground. Gloucestershire had not resisted the Conquest – Bristol, in fact, welcomed Norman rule – and Wulstan, the Bishop of Worcester in whose see much of the county then lay, was one of only two English bishops to stay in office under him. The city's importance is

evident from the fact that the Conqueror's eldest son, Robert Courthose, Duke of Normandy, was buried in what is now Gloucester Cathedral in 1134. His splendid thirteenth-century effigy can still be seen there, while a Norman backgammon set in Gloucester City Museum is another memento from around the time of that Christmas when the Conqueror's visit left an indelible mark on English history.

The Haunted Carollers

One of the most celebrated mass hauntings of the inter-war years came on the evening of 17 December 1937, when a dozen members of the East Compton Prize Band were visited by the White Lady of Over Court, a gaunt and gabled Elizabethan mansion down dark country lanes south-west of the then Gloucestershire village of Almondsbury.

All the band knew the legend of the White Lady, but they had visited Over Court for years without mishap. Even John Purnell, aged 14, was a veteran of half a dozen previous visits, and as the musicians lit their lantern and crunched up the drive just after seven o'clock any talk of spooks was strictly tongue-in-cheek. Minutes later they staggered away convinced that they had seen the apparition, while John Purnell believed he had seen two spirits. It was nearly fifty years later, while watching television, that he learned the truth about one of them.

The East Compton bandsmen who spotted the White Lady of
Over Court in 1937; this fine press photograph was taken a few
days after the event.

He was on the outer edge of the group, and it was during
the second verse of *Hark! The Herald Angels Sing* that he
allowed his gaze to wander along the front of the building.

'At the left hand corner was a tree,' he recalls, 'and I became
aware of a figure standing at the side of it – very tall, white but
not shining, and with a shape I could not describe. It
disappeared, then reappeared before finally vanishing.

'I waited to see the reaction of my companions, but nobody
mentioned it. They could not have seen it, and I knew that if
I'd said I had seen the White Lady they would have treated it as
a huge joke. The best thing to do was keep quiet.

'We completed our carols and trudged back through the
entrance arch – until I suddenly realised that everybody had

The now demolished Over Court, near Almondsbury, *c.* 1910.
The White Lady was seen to the right of the clock tower,
which still stands today.

stopped. In the tangle of undergrowth, hedge and trees to the
left the full moon was throwing odd shadows – but it could
not obscure the fact that there was a bright white figure less
than the length of a cricket pitch away.'

According to another account the band's lantern went out
just before the sighting. One of the younger members shouted
'look there, through the gap', and the figure of the White Lady
was seen floating just above the ground, with a distinctive
bluish glow radiating from it.

'It was about the size of an average person with a tall,
pointed head-dress, and it moved in a zig-zag manner away
from us,' John Purnell recalls. 'It appeared to go behind trees
and through a hedge as we watched. Moving further away it
became smaller, until it finally disappeared. I suppose the
episode lasted about 30 seconds. For several moments nobody
moved, until someone broke the spell with: "Well, I'll be
damned."

'Keeping a little closer together, we continued our carols at a few small cottages. A local farmer stopped his car and shouted: "What's the matter with the band tonight?"

'"We've seen the White Lady," we chorused.

'"Aye, it sounds like it," he replied, driving off in gales of laughter.

'This was the first time a whole group of people had seen the phantom; the local papers reported it, there was a lot of talk at the time, and then it passed into local folklore.'

The White Lady is said to be the wife of an early owner of Over Court, shot by her husband for having an affair with a member of a prominent local family. She staggered wounded from the house to the fish pond at the bottom of the garden and drowned – and it is from there that she is believed to rise and stalk the grounds. I hardly need add that when seen by the band she was heading directly for the pond – through undergrowth so thick that when some of the braver young lads went back to the scene a couple of days later they found it impossible to penetrate.

Over Court's history after this haunting was not a happy one. There was a bizarre death in the fish pond, the house fell empty and became a target for vandals, and in the early 1980s it was eventually demolished after a fire. Modern houses now stand on the site, but the distinctive clock tower remains.

And what of the other ghost that night in the week before Christmas, 1937 – the one seen only by 14-year-old John Purnell?

'I was watching a television programme about deer a couple of years ago,' he says. 'It showed how, in winter, they will stand on their hind legs to strip trees for food. Something clicked. It was exactly the shape I had seen at the side of Over Court all those years ago. There had been white deer on the estate, so my private phantom was well and truly laid to rest. As for the one we all saw, though – I'm still watching TV, but I've seen nothing like it yet.'

from

The Blacksmith's Daughter

SUSAN OLDACRE

Susan Oldacre's discovery of the diaries of Ann Staight, who lived from 1855 to 1892, led to the publication of an absorbing biography in 1985. Ann's village was Dumbleton, in the Vale of Evesham between the North Cotswold fringes and Bredon Hill, and she was 27 at the time of these extracts. Ten years later Ann was dead – in circumstances that give the book a tragic final twist.

Preparations for Christmas were, unlike now, contained within the few days preceding Christmas Day: ' Monday Dec. 18 (1882). Sis went up to Joe's to see the large beast they killed yesterday.'

Inspecting animal carcases may not sound too Christmassy, but 'the large beast' would supply Christmas meals for Joe's customers. Free beef for the tenants from the Hall was an expected, and welcome, part of Christmas. On St. Thomas's Day (December 21) there were more preparations. The church bells rang early: they *stopped* at 5.30 a.m.! Sarah had been inveigled by Mrs. Willoughby Jones into decorating the church for Christmas, and after examining the windows for which she would be responsible she set off into the shrubbery to collect the traditional evergreens, yew, ivy, laurel and holly.

The front room, not much used except for Sunday singing round the piano, was prepared: Tom swept out the chimney and the four 'children' carried the carpet outside for a good beating. Ann's mother grated nutmegs, cut peel and stoned plums for her Christmas puddings, though traditionally plum puddings were made earlier than this. Stir-up Sunday at the end of November is so called because its Collect (the 25th Sunday after Trinity) begins 'Stir up, we beseech Thee, O Lord', and also because it was the time, just before Advent, to stir the Christmas puddings.

Ann rode with Tom and John to Evesham in Joe's trap to greet the Biscoes: 'Mrs. B and Annie came safely, former looking very sadly, but Annie better. We took the luggage to Railway Hotel, then went into the town shopping. Annie went with Tom to buy his overcoat. Tom called in at Mr. Morris's to try to get calves' feet for Joe, but they had none.' It was nearly dark when they reached home at half past five.

It was Mrs. Biscoe's first Christmas without her husband, and a sad one for her, but she and Annie helped Sarah with her church work, and she was generous with gifts: 'Mrs. B gave me a sweet pretty gold watch and chain, and to Sis she gave a lovely bracelet, and Annie gave us a dear little bracelet each from Mrs. Young.' Annie also gave Ann a photograph of 'her dear old home'. Numerous Christmas cards were despatched. Christmas Eve fell on a Sunday that year, and after church 'poor Mrs. Biscoe very low and sad, so when we came out we went through shady walk, and down road she soon felt better.'

Ann and Annie made pikelets for tea, and there was a musical evening with Joe and Louie, Leslie and Cormell: 'We had a nice lot of music. Annie sang some of her Sacred Songs. C.M. and L.L. went before 10, the others soon after. Mrs. B and us three girls sat talking till nearly 12, after the rest were in bed. Heard the bells ring out midnight peal.

'Xmas Day, Dec 25, 1882 . . . Father and boys busy making toast-and-ale, and Mother and Sis seeing to the cooking. Annie and I went to church with the men-folks.

O come all ye faithful
Joyful and triumphant . . .'

In *Silas Marner* (1861) George Eliot described a Christmas morning very similar to this one: 'The church was fuller than all through the rest of the year, with red faces among the abundant dark green boughs – faces prepared for a longer service than usual by an odorous breakfast of toast and ale. Those green boughs, the hymn and anthem never heard but at Christmas – even the Athanasian Creed – brought a vague exulting sense. . .'

Even on Christmas Day there was a postal delivery, with cards for both girls. Joe and Louie and their friend Alf Goodall, another butcher, arrived for Christmas lunch of hare and sirloin beef:

'We had dinner rather late. Gave Mrs. D's maid her dinner, Mrs. D had hers from Rectory. After we had cleared (Sis made fire in parlour), us girls washed and dressed and put on our best. Sis and I wore our jewellery presents (Annie gave us a pair of mittens each, and to the boys she gave two pretty boxes of matches). Annie helped us get tea, all the "boys" went up to Joe's to see after the cattle before tea; Louie, Alf, Sis, Tom and John went to church, Father went with Joe to his house. Annie and I washed up and cleared away, then came upstairs and she read "The Letters" to me. L.L. came before the others were back . . . Later on, the mummers came, and we had them in the kitchen to act, I did some writing in D. the while. . . .'

And after the mummers, the local band! On Boxing Day

morning 'the Toddington band came, and played several tunes. Annie and John had a dance or two, I tried, and Alf and Sis.' There was much music, to Ann's delight. Annie gave her, and occasionally John, long music lessons. They were, after all, a sizeable group of musicians – Ann, Annie, John and Louie all played the piano. Charles sometimes played, but from Ann's comment on another occasion, not very well: 'Pap opened piano and said he'd have a tune, hadn't tried for so long, so he made a noise for a bit.' In addition, Tom, Annie and Louie sang solos, and all joined in singing the hymns and songs.

New Year's Eve, 1882, was a Sunday, as Christmas Eve had been. Ann and Annie went to church with the boys, where they listened to a sermon on a text familiar from the funerals they had attended: 'So teach us to number our days' (Psalm 90, verse 12).

'Annie played and sang till supper-time . . . then us two went aloft and did a lot of talking, and I wrote a bit. Boys came up for bed, and pushed in to see what we were doing, and we had a rare "scrimmage" and shouting. They tried to get at desk, but Sis came to the rescue, and we beat them. Father and Mother followed the boys to bed, us four sat up and read till the bells began ringing Old Year out and New One in. Some men came to the back door wishing us Happy New Year, but we put out the light till they were gone, then went to bed after drinking healths and exchanging good wishes.'

1882 had been a year of sharp contrasts. It had begun with Ann a barmaid in a busy town close to London; it ended with her sequestered again in a small village remote from any city. Despite the sadness of the year – the deaths of Annie's father, Louie's brother, Louie's baby, Sarah Young's bridegroom – it had been a happy and healthy one for Ann and her family and it ended in an ideal way, Christmas spent among loved ones and friends.

The School Concert

HUMPHREY PHELPS

Humphrey Phelps wrote this reminiscence in 1976, looking back some seven or eight years to his youngest son's primary school days. Today he is still very much in touch with concerts and nativity plays through his grandchildren.

It is a week before Christmas. I am working in the barn and trying to hurry. From where I work I catch glimpses of my wife, who keeps coming out of the house and looking about. I know she is looking for me, but I keep just out of sight and increase my pace. If she sees me she will call me in, but I want to finish my job first.

My haste and her looking about are because of the school concert this afternoon. We want to arrive early to find good seats; the school is always packed for its concert. We eat our lunch quickly, eyes on the clock, and then I run upstairs to wash and change. My wife, ready before lunch and impatient to be off, keeps shouting: 'Hurry up, we shall be late.' An annoying habit; I'm sure it only slows me up, making me fumble with buttons and tie.

We arrive in fine time. The original building is of mellow brick, but two new classrooms have been added. The main

Fairies, Father Christmas, and other characters swathed in mystery: the Christmas play at St. James' School, Chipping Campden, in 1905.

room is gay with decorations. Paper chains hang from the ceiling, and the whole school is festooned with the children's work. On the walls are their cheerful, uninhibited paintings. They get a real education here; the headmaster stimulates their interest, invests them with a zest for learning and living. And above all, music; the school resounds with music and song.

The children are full of excitement, the concert today, the party tomorrow, then holidays and Christmas. It is infectious and soon we parents, too, are in festive mood. The headmaster and the two teachers enter. Immediately the children become subdued and orderly, but the buzz of chatter from the parents continues until the headmaster claps his hands and bids us welcome.

The smallest children perform a simple play, and then they

sing. Everybody applauds, except a stocky little boy who boos loudly. The headmaster turns quickly and asks: 'Who did that?' But he knows well enough who it was, and tells the culprit: 'Come here and sit by me and behave yourself.'

The middle class perform their play. Rupert, our youngest son, is Uncle John, a seafaring man, who takes the children to see how Christmas is spent in other lands. As he puts his arm round them in avuncular fashion and speaks his lines loud and clear I feel a lump in my throat; and so does my wife, she tells me later.

And then it's the turn of the older children, who perform a short version of *A Christmas Carol*. The headmaster is narrator. He has the actor's well modulated voice. Twice I've seen him play Macbeth, and doubt if I'll ever see a better portrayal.

Half a dozen of the older children play violins, their faces intent and serious, the girls' hair almost in danger of becoming entangled amid bow and strings. Next, the younger ones play recorders. Their eyes stare from the effort of concentration, but one feels that at any moment they may cease their blowing and start to laugh.

Finally, the whole school sing carols, their childish voices soft and clear. The headmaster plays the piano. It is a joy to hear, a pleasure to watch. The other two teachers are obviously enjoying themselves; it's that kind of school, busy and happy. I would like to catch and hold this scene, and the children's sweet tones; it is a delight close to tears.

On Christmas Leave

W. W. BLAIR-FISH

This poem, about coming home to Blockley from the trenches of France, was first published in 'Punch' on 27 December 1916. In my view it warrants inclusion in any anthology of First World War verse, for it rings true where the works of many a more celebrated poet sound a false note. Blair-Fish was a journalist who lived in part of the Manor House and wrote short plays for the local amateur dramatic society after the war. Chainey, the landlord of the Crown, did indeed run a horse-drawn bus between the village and the railway station, while the retired military man was Major Spencer, then agent for the Northwick estate.

When I got into Chainey's bus
Down at the station it began;
I didn't seem a fighting man
No more: the old hills made no fuss
At seeing me; the winding road
That troops and transports never knowed,
And the old station nag's click-clack
Just took me back.

The Twelve Apostles' boughs were bare,
Just as they was last time I came.
Mother was looking just the same

And father hadn't turned a hair.
I washed as usual at the pump;
My bed had got the same old lump;
Dick lived next door – I near forgot
I seen him shot.

Church wasn't changed on Christmas Day –
Old Westmacott took round the plate;
The old Major stood up stiff and straight
And it seemed somehow just like play
Saluting him, retired an' all.
Home – No, the war I think – seems small. . .
This evening I go back to France
And take my chance.

Country Christmas

LEONARD CLARK

This reminiscence comes from Leonard Clark's collection
Green Wood, *first published in 1962. Besides his
national repute as a writer of children's poetry, Clark,
who was brought up in Cinderford, was known widely in
Gloucestershire and the Cotswolds as a lively and devoted
schools inspector. He wrote four volumes of autobio-
graphical essays, all of which were reissued by Dobson*

· A Cotswold Christmas ·

Books in the 1970s. No primitive, he looked back on his early years with imagination and skill, and at its best his writing is as absorbing and evocative as Laurie Lee's.

I have many vivid memories of the Christmases which I spent, as a child, in the country. At this distance of time they seem to have been never-ending, their delights as fresh today as yesterday. Christmas is a festival of mystery, of suspense, of waiting, as it were, on the half edge of the dark. It is as mysterious as Easter, which is not surprising, for both festivals of the Christian year are concerned with the twin enigmas of birth and death. And nowhere is Christmas more mysterious than in the country, where one is surrounded by silence, and by fields and hills which remember every Christmas that has ever been.

The countryside of my childhood was made up of many diverse elements. I lived in daily sight of trees, trees so black against the white landscape that I imagined them to be the same trees of the forests in the fairy tales. From the top of the winter mushroom of a long hill which stretched itself into the dun skies I could see, on a clear day, the slow Severn moving out to sea, the far-away Cathedral at Gloucester as De Wint painted it, and miles of squares and oblongs that were the valley fields levelled by the first fall of snow. Christmas in such a countryside gained, for me, an added mystery and purity. The peaceful land was itself the essence of the season.

One of my recollections is of a Christmas Eve when Mother and I were waiting for my brother to arrive from London. We sat in our kitchen, bright with holly and ivy and smelling sweet from the paraffin lamp, before a fire which, glutted with logs, blazed its glory half-way up the chimney. The lamp shed its soft crystal light on the tablecloth upon which had been laid a late supper of bread and cheese, butter and home-made chutney. The beauty of that table was in its simplicity, and it

The old Bell Inn in Bisley, March 1916.

Skating on Toadsmoor Lake at Brimscombe in 1908. It was
frozen on two successive Sundays in January, and the people of
Stroud flocked out on the railcars.

was not for nothing that a Christmas rose had been placed in a blue china vase just at that spot where the light finished and the dark began.

Mother yawned over her knitting, the fat tabby cat, with greedy anticipations of the morrow, had become a fire-worshipper. The plum puddings spluttered their steaming songs on the newly black-leaded hob. Outside, the night was as still as the room inside. Two deep silences had merged into the one silence of Christmas night. I was waiting for something to happen, waiting, perhaps, for something more than the arrival of my brother. Would he come, I thought, like a thief in the night, or would he call to us when he got within earshot of the house?

The grandfather clock ticked on. The warm cat dreamed in her sleep. I sat in my nightclothes, hands clasped together round my knees, face flushed, and my head of golden curls mingling its carbolic with the smell of the lamp. Once or twice I looked through the frosted window-panes to see a single star. Perhaps, I said to myself, this was the very star that, poor innocent, had strayed out of time and place. Maybe it would lead my brother as it led those other men. And he would find the same things at *his* journey's end as *they* did at theirs: peace and a waiting child.

I can remember how, suddenly, we heard the click of the latch of the gate, and then quick footsteps crunching the powdered snow. We both rose to our feet in all expectancy. 'Is that you?' said Mother. 'It's him,' I shouted, forgetting my grammar in the tide of feeling that swept over me. The door opened, broken icicles tinkled on the stone paving, and there was my brother. I can see him now. He was slender, black-coated as fitted a grocer's journeyman going home to his native place, with bowler hat, deep collar and bootlace tie, and a wicker travelling basket lashed, so it seemed to my sleepy eyes, to his right hand.

Of course there were huggings and kissings and greetings. Words flew faster than snowflakes. The quiet of the kitchen was punctured by a hundred questions and fifty answers. He told us how he had caught the train at Paddington just as the London dark was falling, how twice he had gone to sleep, only to wake and find a whitening world moving ever more quickly past him. Then he had found himself at the almost deserted main-line station, four miles from our home, and had walked up over the solid fields until he had reached the village.

'What have you got for me?' I asked, and he: 'You wait till tomorrow, young fellow.' But for Mother he could not curb himself. He opened his wicker basket and then, fumbling amongst the dirty linen, produced a small tin of lobster. This, then, was his gift, and curiously enough it had come from the East, a tin of lobster, from son to mother. Mother said 'We'll have that tomorrow,' though I suspect she was itching to sample it immediately.

Now if he had brought lobster for Mother, I conjectured, what would there be for me? I had visions of tins of condensed milk, lengths of aromatic angelica, Jordan almonds and Smyrna figs. The cat looked up eagerly with the kind of expression which said 'And what for me?' as, no doubt, ox and ass in the old cobwebbed barn had gazed in expectation at the shining faces of the three kings. 'Now to bed, all of you,' said Mother. She blew out the lamp, fed the fire, pacified the cat, and then we all left the kitchen for upstairs. I thought: 'I wonder who will enter next.'

I lit my stump of candle by the simple process of holding it against the hot bars of the grate, a method of ignition which, though obvious to me, for some obscure domestic reason always irritated my mother. Long shadows appeared like uninvited strangers on the whitewashed walls, their shapes like no other shapes on earth, though occasionally they photographed in grey, grotesque exaggerations of various things about the room. The shadows followed me when I began the terrifying ascent of the linoleumed stairs to my bedroom. But, by some midnight necromancy, their shapes were changed again on the ceiling that descended lower and lower as I climbed higher and higher.

Eventually I succeeded in scaling the winding, precipitous slopes, and there was the grained and varnished door which led to my bedroom. I placed the sulky candle on the marble-topped washstand, and after a final glance at star and snow, got into bed. The shadows changed their shapes again on all four walls. They looked like holly leaves or jagged Himalayan peaks. When a gust of wind rocked the candle flame the shadows became volcanic and menacing. Soon, like a god, I turned light into dark, by simply placing a matchbox on top of the candle.

All sounds died to nothingness in the house. Tom Williams's horse neighed two fields away. The last echoes of *Hail, Smiling Morn* faded with the sound of country feet. I felt that the whole world was waiting, that everybody was pretending to be asleep, that new life was working in air and soil. Only the constant skies kept silent watch. I lay rigid in the white-blanketed coffin of the bed with the smell of the frost about me, until sleep had robbed me of further imaginings.

I woke to the sound of the church clock telling me it was eight or seven or six, for I could not be sure that I had heard its first striking. But the light was there, and the world outside my window was new and shining. There were diamonds in trees, silver on roads and best of all, a blood-red robin, first trumpeter of Christmas morning. Old William Godbeer, our milkman, unseen but faithful, was rattling from door to door. Mother was already at work in the kitchen. Would there be the customary boiled egg for breakfast, I wondered. Was it really Christmas morning? And there, hanging like a dislocated black limb, was my stocking at the bottom of the bed.

So he had not forgotten me. But his coming and his kindness were as much a mystery as ever. Who had told him that I wanted *Treasure Island,* and what would my mother have said if she had seen the way he had stretched my stocking? The apple and orange, whose cold faces I warmed against my nightgown, I had half expected. But would the knife have that thing for getting out the stones in horses' hooves? Of course I had to nibble a few black inches of liquorice bootlaces, I had to see if the triple-coloured belt had the snake buckle on it, and I simply had to look at the date on the two shilling piece so neatly wrapped up in rustling tissue paper. How did he manage to get it all in, and how did he know?

Soon, hastily dressed and even more hastily washed, I clattered down the stairs and burst into the kitchen with the shrillest of 'Merry Christmases' to my mother and brother. The recollection of those Christmas Day breakfasts has long departed, but I suppose they were just the same kind of breakfasts which were being enjoyed at a thousand other tables on that particular morning. However, I can remember the red jersey which Mother had knitted for me, the gaudily decorated tin of London humbugs which my brother gave to me, and myself, shyly presenting him with a large bottle of the best brilliantine, and her with 'a solid gold ring with a real diamond in it'.

I had the vain belief that in giving her this piece of jewellery I might make more beautiful the already beautiful. The trouble about the ring was that I had given no thought as to its size. My difficulty had been price. After many painful and unsuccessful attempts to force it over obstinate and rheumatic knuckles, it landed safely on a piece of tinsel round her neck, and finally came to rest on gently-heaving black bombazine. 'It's lovely,' she said, 'and I'm glad you gave me gold on a Christmas morning.'

My brother was already sniffing the imprisoned incense of

the brilliantine. He would look like a king in his grocer's shop three days hence. And I shall always be grateful to him for politely placing his thumb over the pencilled 7½d. which, by some unfortunate miscalculation, had forced its vulgar way between the words 'Finest' and 'Perfumed'.

The bell was already ringing for church. I raced down the hill, rushed round to the vestry door and was just in time to put on my newly-laundered surplice, which, after several mistakes, I managed to get the right way round. Our blind organist was already giving a good imitation of Christmas bells up in his loft. The verger was fussing with the lamps. The bidding prayer was said, and then a dozen country choirboys filed out into their stalls.

The whole building seemed like a forest; there was so much holly about that even the members of the congregation seemed to be sprouting it. Then came the great moment. We gulped down our last sugared almond and, after the diapasons had rolled out from the organ, we let the morning air have it in full measure. Charles, our organist, had Christmas at his mercy. The Vicar, white-bearded like an Old Testament patriarch, smiled on his flock, and we, the twelve devils and angels of the choir, lifted up our voices and sang 'Hark, the herald angels sing', and, as if that were not enough, followed it with 'Glory to the new-born King'. Mendelssohn, no doubt, placed fingers on his heavenly ears, but we gave him and Heaven no respite, for we told both that God and sinners had been reconciled. We informed Evan Harris, Mary Downs, Tom Nicholas and all the rest of the congregation that Christ was born in Bethlehem, and would give them second birth.

The day had other delights to follow, but though none of us could put the proper words to it, we knew that, in that spot and at that moment in time, waiting had been rewarded and that a child had been born.

Christmas, Swinging '66

The night before Christmas Eve in 1987 I was in a bar just off the High Street in Cheltenham. There was the usual pre-Christmas scrummage of people, but by far the most noise was coming from two or three tables in the corner, where a dozen men aged about forty were talking and laughing uproariously.

It turned out to be a reunion, the result of one of those usually drunken occasions when everyone in the room pledges to meet up again so many years hence. I have been party to one or two in the past, but nothing has ever come of them. In this case, however, one of the number had taken it all very seriously, beavered away for months chasing up last known addresses and elderly parents, and the jolly little band in the corner was the result.

Their last time together had been Christmas, 1966. Christmas in Cheltenham in 1966 had been magic, one of them told me. Of the handful of times in his life when he had truly believed he was in the right place at the right time, none meant more to him than being nineteen in Cheltenham in 1966. From what the lads had been saying to him tonight, they felt exactly the same way.

As I was not nineteen in Cheltenham in 1966, I checked the local newspapers of December that year to see what all the fuss was about. At the end of it I was little the wiser. I know that year was special for members of the post-war baby boom generation, all then aged about twenty. The Swinging England youth culture was at its height, before the responsibilities of jobs, marriage and children took their toll of most of them, and the drugs and disillusionment of fading flower-power accounted for the rest. But reading the papers, with their news of the deaths of local worthies, W.I. meetings and corner shop break-ins, there was little to suggest a bright new dawning.

You could buy a holiday in Lloret from Hourmont for £34 10s., a three-piece suite from Whites of Pittville Street for $59\frac{1}{2}$ guineas, a Christmas dance and buffet supper at Burleigh Court, Brimscombe for 18s. 6d. and a bottle of whisky from Peter Dominic at 46s. 11d. If you wanted to treat yourself to a car for Christmas, Imperial Motors of Montpellier Spa Road had a three-year-old Jaguar E-Type for £1,025, while P. B. Bailey of Cleeve Hill Garage was offering 10,000 Green Shield Stamps on all used vehicles priced above £100.

Nationally, Harold Wilson's Government, re-elected with an increased majority during a year that also saw England's footballers win the World Cup, was struggling through crises that saw Ian Smith declare Rhodesia independent after the failure of peace talks on the cruiser *Tiger* in the Mediterranean, pressure on the pound and unemployment rising to what was seen as a politically damaging 500,000-plus. The acrimonious Aberfan disaster inquiry was another depressing running story.

A big human interest tale that December was the pop musician Jet Harris's claim for damages after a crash on the road between Pershore and Evesham three years previously. He was eventually awarded a little over £11,000, but to win it his counsel was forced to paint a gloomy picture of his career and personality since the accident, and it must have been a horrendous ordeal for a vulnerable and sensitive man. At the end of the hearing it was announced that Harris's 23-year-old wife Sue, a Plough Hotel barmaid whom he had married at Cheltenham Register Office only a few months earlier, was suing him for divorce. Merry Christmas, Jet.

Elsewhere the Great Train Robber Buster Edwards was gaoled for 15 years, the 65-year-old yachtsman Francis Chichester completed his 107-day voyage from Plymouth to Sydney, and it was announced that there were proposals to replace 'the 10s. note by 50 Newpence'. Plans were unveiled to restore the ten medieval cottages along Church Street, Tewkesbury, close to the Abbey, at a cost of £50,000 – no mean sum when a new detached house at Chalford could be bought for £3,250. Cheltenham's education officer, Mr. L. F. R. Simmonds, took advantage of the Technical High School's speech day to dismiss the 11-plus examination as something akin to the Miss World contest, while the Gloucestershire County Cricket Club secretary Richard McCrudden, who was to die before 1967 was out, called for players to go part-time and for championship matches to be played at weekends only: 'If a man has a job paying £20 a week and he knows he can earn another £20 at the weekend by playing cricket, it becomes an attractive proposition.'

Entertainment that Christmas included different productions of *Dick Whittington* at both the Cheltenham Everyman and the New Theatre, Oxford, where the stars were the Crazy Gang veterans Bud Flanagan, Charlie Naughton and Monsewer Eddie Gray. The big show at the Bristol Hippodrome was *Humpty Dumpty* with the Seekers, who were high in the pop charts with 'Morningtown Ride', while North Cotswold residents were beckoned by the unrelated Frankie and Norman Vaughan in *The Pied Piper* at the Coventry Theatre. In the week before the panto the Everyman was offering the musical *Lock Up Your Daughters*, with Pat Kirkwood and Hubert Gregg, and live panto came to Cheltenham Odeon for a week in January with William Hartnell, TV's first Dr. Who, in *Puss in Boots*.

Perhaps it was just as well, since there was not a lot on at the cinema. In the big cities *The Sound of Music* was grinding relentlessly on, and dubious delights in Cheltenham included *Tarzan the Magnificent* with Gordon Scott at Poole's Coliseum, *Three on a Couch* with Jerry Lewis and Janet Leigh at the ABC and *Beau Geste* at the Odeon. Things looked up a little on Boxing Day, when the ABC brought in Audrey Hepburn and Rex Harrison's enchanting *My Fair Lady*.

As for Swinging England and youth culture, there was little evidence of it in the press. Dear old uncle Acker Bilk from Zummerzet did a gig at Cheltenham Town Hall two days before Christmas, and the changing times were hinted at by an advertisement for the Police Ball at the same venue, where dancing was to the Dance Orchestra of the Royal Tank Regiment (by kind permission of the Colonel's Commandant) – plus Dean Prince and the Dukes.

The big Christmas record of that year was Tom Jones's 'Green, Green Grass of Home', while other hits that live on in the memory included the Beach Boys' 'Good Vibrations', 'Gimme Some Loving' by the Spencer Davis Group, 'Semi-Detached Suburban Mr James by Manfred Mann, and the Four Tops' 'Reach Out I'll Be There'. By far the hottest spot in Cheltenham was the Blue Moon club in the High Street, where December attractions included Zoot Money, a superb London blues band which never achieved outstanding commercial success, and the up-and-coming Birmingham group The Move – billed as 'The Psychodelic Phenomena'. Apart from correcting the spelling of 'Psychodelic' and tidying up the grammar of 'The Phenomena', I'd go along with that.

These, then, were my findings on Christmas 1966. Yet looking at those men in the pub that night, I know there must have been more in the air than this. It just didn't get in the papers, I suppose, like all the best things that ever happen to you in your life.

from

A Cotswold Year

C. HENRY WARREN

Warren settled into life in the Cotswolds after an army and teaching career that had taken him from the Middle East to the Home Counties, and in 1936, four years after his arrival, he chronicled his view of the changing seasons in A Cotswold Year. *Unusually, his year began in December, so he wasted no time in telling his Christmas tale.*

December 23. A 'bus ride in a remote country district is always an adventure, but never quite so much an adventure as just before Christmas. I was out in the heart of the Cotswolds and wanted to get to Cirencester, a journey impossible by train and only possible by 'bus if I could make two awkward connections fit in. All told it was under fifteen miles, but I shouldn't have bumped into such a variety of people in ten times that distance on a train.

At all times rural 'buses are rare provokers of good fellowship: no matter how disgruntled the passengers may be when they get in, before they have gone far they have all been shaken up into such a mood of friendliness and good humour that they seem prepared to tell their neighbours almost anything about their most private lives. But on a day like this, when Christmas is in the air, good fellowship is even more than usually rampant.

69

The first 'bus I got into had been decorated behind the driver's seat with a couple of mistletoe sprays lavish with berries. I suspected the young conductor, for no doubt he was a wit. At one stopping-place in a village a young lady got in, smart in a townish sort of way that somehow didn't fit the scene. The buzz of conversation immediately stopped, and everybody stared at her while she made her way to the only empty seat in the 'bus: it was just behind the driver and under the mistletoe. There was a suppressed giggle or two, and then the young conductor started whistling *If You Were The Only Girl In The World,* and winked knowingly at the rest of us. Everything was a joke to him. Even when one of his name-boards fell off the rack (where he had placed it none too securely) on to a passenger's head, he simply laughed and said: 'I'll let you off with a warning this time!'

The second 'bus was no less festive, though I missed the mistletoe and the gay young conductor. Near me at one time sat a friendly old man who was the very image of (the Prime Minister) Mr. Baldwin. A woman got in, whom he knew. She had on her head what appeared to be a clergyman's flap hat. My neighbour greeted her loudly and cheerily with: 'Good morning! How's the arm?' She paused on her way to her seat, clutched at the nearest support and glared at him. 'It was the foot!' she said indignantly. And when she was seated she launched on a tale of broken bones and accidents and funny feelings and *sal volatile* that lasted until she got out at her destination.

Two boys were having a fine time with a large electric bicycle lamp which they had just bought. It was so large and splendid that they simply couldn't resist flashing it on; so they shone it into one another's mouths to see how far down their throats they could see.

Then there was a pale and serious clergyman who was being taken into the town by his wife to do some shopping. He was one of the shyest men I have ever seen, and obviously embarrassed to find himself jostled about with such a loud lot of people; but his wife was quite oblivious of them. She was very much concerned as to what money she ought to spend on almanacks and suchlike little gifts for the parishioners. Her husband tried to dismiss the matter as quite unimportant; he didn't like talking about such things in front of other people.

I could see from his wife's insistent preoccupation, however, that a few pence more or less mattered a great deal. Theirs was the genteel poverty of those who have a reputation to keep up, and nothing to keep it up on. 'You haven't thrown away the tickets, have you?' she asked him presently, careful of everything by sheer force of habit. 'No, here they are, dear,' he answered meekly, pulling them out of the palm of his dingy suede gloves. And for the remainder of the journey they were silent, unable to bridge the barrier between themselves and their fellow-passengers, the only silent people in the 'bus.

December 24. When we got to Miserden, the village was shut in an intense darkness: no pointed junipers thrust their shadowy outlines against the sky, and only an occasional lamp in somebody's cottage window declared that not everybody was asleep. Most of the menfolk of the village must have been in the Carpenter's Arms, so large an assembly filled the smoke-dense room when we opened the door. There must have been thirty men present, sitting and standing about, talking and laughing, while the landlord hurried in and out among them, throwing a joke over his shoulders as he attended to the orders fired at him from all quarters.

A wood fire filled the large open fireplace, over which there were arranged a row of bright brass candlesticks and some shining steel spits. No game of darts monopolised the space and the conversation; no unsightly beer or tobacco advertisements spoiled the clean, washed walls; and instead of the usual smoky and inadequate oil lamp, a smart petrol lamp threw abundance of light everywhere. I do not know a more attractive inn anywhere in the Cotswolds, and certainly I have never seen one so full of jovial goodwill as the Carpenter's Arms was this evening.

Here were men who preferred sociable talk to silent drinks and games in a corner; even the inevitable 'oldest inhabitant', a man of 86, mingled with the rest, his hand cupping his ear to catch the latest piece of local scandal and his eyes lighting up with pleasure as he bandied racy quips with his friends. Song after song filled the smoke-blue room, everybody joining in with gusto, and quite drowning the impromptu accompaniment of the fiddler, who wandered in and out among the singing crowd, shutting his eyes and sweeping his bow up to the ceiling. Now and then one of the men would sing a solo, while the fiddler stood at his side and the rest of the company joined heartily in the chorus.

One of the best songs tonight was a masterly performance of *The Barley Mow* and how good it was to hear this grand old folk song removed from the artificial atmosphere of the drawing room or festival and sung by men who have lived the sentiments they were singing! But perhaps my fancy was most seized by a ballad I had never heard before. It was sung by a middle-aged man whose absence of any tonal sense was more than compensated for by a rare vigour and naturalness.

His ballad was all about a man who sailed abroad, taking with him a wonderful bird in a gilded cage. When he had settled down in his new country, obviously one of our colonies, the men used to gather about him to listen to the singing of that bird, their hearts almost ceasing to beat at hearing again a thrush from their own far-away homeland. . .

Too soon the landlord called 'Time, gentlemen!' For a while we stood outside the door in the pitch-black night tidying up the tag-ends of conversation, then made for home. 'Goodnight, Bill! Goodnight, Jack! And a happy Christmas!'

from

The Diary of a Victorian Squire

DEARMAN BIRCHALL

Dearman Birchall was a wealthy Leeds merchant who moved to the edge of the Cotswolds at Bowden Hall, Upton St. Leonards in 1868. He threw himself heartily into the life of the village squire, and the Christmas entries of his diary, edited by the late David Verey and published in 1983, reflect both the social and public life of a respected member of the Gloucestershire county set.

1870

Dec 17. Hunted with the Cotteswolds. The meet was at the Kennels at Cheltenham and we rode on the magnificent downs on the summit of Cleeve Hill. We passed by Postlip Hall and had a famous gallop.

Dec 20. Meet at Fretherne Court. Found in covert behind the House. Soon lost; but picked up another at Withy Bed, Frampton. Ran him with great speed to within 2 miles of Sharpness Point, a fine sight on the sands. A most enjoyable day, 9 hours in the saddle, about 40 miles.

The Boxing Day meet, Tockington Green, *c.* 1905.

Dec 21. Conversazione at Cirencester – Constable's – very pleasant evening. Prof. Church lectured on the colour and copper obtained from the Touraco's wing, another gentleman on deep sea dredgings, especially new sponges. The exhibition of jewellery of the 17th century was much admired. Constable astonishes with the boldness of his ideas and general liberality of sentiment.

Dec 27. Clara's Christmas Tree at Upton School, with Moody Bell's Magic Lantern; latter very poor, but the evening was a delightful one. All our neighbours assisted, and the tree was a genuine success, 148 bringing, with extra ones, the presents up to about 200.

Dec 30. Party charades at the Hyetts at Painswick (House). Francis Hyett, Mr. Dickinson, Miss Wolley, Mr. Wallace and Miss Hyett acted *Slasher and Crasher,* a very amusing play; but the finest fun was in an exhibition of automaton wax works, the Marquis of Lorne and Princess Louise kissing hands especially good, and Miss Wolley's singing a Chinese song accompanying herself on a banjo infinitely amusing.

All the week the pond has been frozen and we have had large parties of skaters. As many as a dozen came in to lunch one day, including the Sumners. On Wednesday we sat down 14 to dinner, Miss Somerset and Georgie and the Ackers etc.; nothing could go off better.

1871

Jan 4. The Gambier Parrys' ball (at Highnam Court), a mixture of juveniles and adults. The dancing was most spirited and I danced with a very pretty girl, a Miss Noel, also with two Misses Guise and Carrie Somerset. Amy (Birchall's sister-in-law through his marriage to his late first wife) was very giddy during the Lancers, but I attribute it more to the heat of the room than to anything else. She enjoyed the party and seemed quite well afterwards. On our way home she confessed her penchant for the Rev. Mr. Berry, whom she met in Northampton.

Dec 22. Feast at the school. Christmas Tree was covered with salt by Miss Van to represent snow, but it sadly spoiled the presents underneath.

Dec 25. Eliza, Clara (Birchall's older half-sister and nine-year-old daughter) and I dined alone. The weather was wet and nasty. Eliza felt much for poor Sophy and William who have lost their little girl from pneumonia, and who seem sadly distressed.

Improvements at Bowden during the winter were an additional grape house, backed by a raising house with heating water apparatus to supply both old and new houses. The pond showing signs of giving way and leaking heavily in the low or southern side, I set about and had the water let off and the whole fresh puddled to make it more secure, and to prevent injury from the effects of the swans dashing about, I had it all coated in the south side with a facing of stone.

Dec 31. Walked home with Col. and Mrs. Somerset. They told me Georgie (their daughter) was defiant, praised her as being an angel; but lamented she was going to throw herself away on an adventurer. From Philadelphia they have received news that he is not known as a Count, but as a business man. When he left he was in debt, and writs and warrants have been issued against him during the last month.

He is not known in society in England. He assumed the title, finding that a card with 'Count' paid amongst the English. Col. Somerset does not think that he has any right to the title. Georgie says when they thought he was rich and had a title they urged her to marry him. 'I agreed with reluctance. When I find he is poor I stick to him. If I do find he is worthless it will be my mission in life to reform him.' So the melancholy sacrifice is to be consummated on Thursday, because no-one can come forward and prevent a steady young lady from throwing herself on a regular scape-grace.

Although he does not admit it here, Birchall was among those of the Somersets' circle who were immediately captivated by the self-styled Count d'Epineul. His diary entry for 13 September 1871 read: 'Dined at Dr. Ancrum's to meet Count d'Epineul, a marvellous fellow reminding one strongly of the Count of Monte Christo. In spite of his recent illness, which had caused him to faint twice today, he was the life of the party and amongst plenty of play and wonderful tricks he caused umbrellas and sticks to stand both perpendicularly and obliquely on the carpet without touching. I never was more surprised in my life.'

Christmas

JIM TURNER

*This second poem by Jim Turner of Cirencester saw him in
a more reflective mood, sensing in the Cotswold winter
countryside a religious presence that predates Christianity.*

With leaves winged wide, the pagan mistletoe
Hangs lucent pearls beneath the blackened beam.
Bright-beaded holly fringes every ledge
And clinging ivy crowns the mirror's shine.

At midnight mass the white-coped, ageing priest
Intones the Christmas gospel to the dark,
Drops the light wafer into proffered palm
And lowers the silver chalice to cold lips.

Day finds the wold new-white from sky to sky,
Deep ditches level in the hollow lane,
Gates three-bar-deep beside the sleeping farm
Where birds beg dumbly for small charity.

Pagan and Christian, interweaving still,
Marry the ancient dread with new-born hope.
Winter's endurance promises the spring,
New-leaved, fresh-flowered, the resurrected year.

Pickwick in Tewkesbury

Successive owners of the Royal Hop Pole Hotel in Tewkesbury have made much, over the years, of the fact that Samuel Pickwick and his cronies stopped to dine there in Charles Dickens's early novel *The Pickwick Papers* (1836–37), more correctly titled 'The Posthumous Papers of the Pickwick Club'. It is not surprising that they make the most of it, and I understand why many people link the incident with Christmas, for both stagecoaches and Dickens have strong associations with this time of year.

The truth is, however, that in my copy of the book, which runs to 639 pages of dense type, the Tewkesbury halt accounts for just over three lines; the vehicle was not a stagecoach but a two-seater chaise; and the journey took place in high summer, allowing the party to travel on to Birmingham that evening before total darkness fell.

The chaise was drawn by a pair of horses with a postillion riding the left-hand one. Pickwick and Sam Weller left their hotel in Bristol promptly at 8.45 that morning, the first task being to pick up Ben Allen from Bob Sawyer's house. The idea was for Allen to join Pickwick in the coach and for Weller to ride in the dickey-seat at the back, but Sawyer threw all plans into chaos by insisting on coming along, too.

Already in an apparently over-boisterous mood, even at such an early hour, he squeezed himself into an old coat several sizes too small for him, and as soon as the streets of Bristol were left

Mr. Pickwick and his merry band head north from Bristol.

behind he swapped hats with Weller, tied a huge red handkerchief to the rear of the coach, had fun making bugle noises and was up on the roof with a bottle in one hand and a large sandwich in the other before Pickwick knew what was happening. Weller contented himself with a sandwich alone in the dickey.

Pickwick restored a little decorum and the party headed up what we now know as the A38. At 11.30 they reached the Bell at Berkeley Heath – now no longer an inn – and Sawyer saw the stop to change horses there as the ideal excuse for an early lunch.

'Why, we have only come nineteen miles, and have eighty-seven and a half to go,' Pickwick protested.

'Just the reason why we should take something to enable us to bear up against the fatigue,' Sawyer replied.

He ordered 'everything they have cold, on the table', bottled ale and the best Madeira, and Pickwick and Allen soon entered into the spirit of things, while Weller presumably made himself at home in the servants' kitchen. By the time they left, Pickwick was quite happy for Sawyer to make his bugle noises and wave his red flag, and they took with them 'the best substitute for milk-punch that could be procured on so short a notice'.

It must have been mid-afternoon when they reached Tewkesbury. Dickens makes not the slightest mention of the journey between the two points – his characters were his prime concern, not the topography of only vaguely-known West Country roads – and immediately after the Berkeley Heath stop comes the incident on which the proprietors of the Royal Hop Pole have been dining out for more than 150 years:

'At the Hop Pole at Tewkesbury, they stopped to dine; upon which occasion there was more bottled ale, with some more Madeira, and some Port besides; and here the case-bottle was replenished for the fourth time. Under the influence of these combined stimulants, Mr. Pickwick and Mr. Ben Allen fell fast asleep for thirty miles, while Bob and Mr. Weller sang duets in the dickey.'

And that's it. By the time Pickwick wakes up it is dark and they are on the outskirts of Birmingham, they go about their errand of meeting Nathaniel Winkle's father, and the huge

Tewkesbury's Royal Hop Pole Hotel in the 1980s, still proud
of its links with Pickwick.

picaresque novel sprawls on for another 70 pages. None of
which stops me from trying to be in Tewkesbury at this time
of year, having a drink at the Hop Pole and thinking of old
Pickwick rolling up there in a great Christmas-card stagecoach
with holly in his hat. Sometimes fantasy is better than reality,
even when you're dealing with a master story-teller like
Dickens.

Two Festive Recipes

CAROL WRIGHT

In her Cotswolds contribution to the Cassell's 'Country Cookbook' series, published in 1975, Carol Wright threw herself wholeheartedly into researching the traditions behind local speciality dishes from all times of the year. Here she gives a drink recipe from the wassailing days immediately before Christmas and an old country favourite from Twelfth Night.

Wotton-under-Edge lies in the south-west corner of the Cotswolds, a village like many in this area clinging tenuously to an escarpment of the hills, so steep that the bedrooms of houses are often at road level. Its name means 'wool town', a key to the area. Woad once grew there well. In the grammar school built in 1832 Isaac Pitman (of shorthand fame) was a master. Below in sheltered valleys, once separate worlds from the villages in the next vale, other villages lie in areas known as 'bottoms'; Ozleworth Bottom is close to Wotton. Half way between Wotton and Dursley is Waterley Bottom, which has given its name to a group of mummers.

Since medieval times, mummers have toured villages at Christmas time, acting out old allegorical plays. Today the Waterley Bottom Mummers are a group of young teachers who have resurrected a traditional play and perform it around the pubs of the area at Christmas, properly demanding as their fee a bowl of wassail to drink. As the performance takes only

82

A Cotswold kitchen at Cogges Farm Museum, Witney.

The Waterley Bottom Mummers, great favourites in the pubs
around Dursley.

about twenty minutes the mummers get very jolly by the end
of the evening.

The Waterley wassail bowl, with four handles, is made in
wood by a local craftsman; it is copied from a traditional one
found at Tresham, near Wotton, in which an old lady grew
geraniums. **Wassail Cup** is not a punch. In the eighteenth
century a recipe used 1 lb. of brown sugar, a pint of hot water,
grated nutmeg, a large lump of chopped preserved ginger
root, four glasses of sherry and five pints of cold beer. A little
yeast was spread on hot slices of toast and added. The mixture
stood for several hours before it was bottled and after a few
days, when the corks were popping out, it was poured into the
wassail bowl and served with hot roasted apples floating in it.

At Christmas in Gloucester youngsters used to carry a

spiced ale bowl from house to house and chant:

Wassail! Wassail! All over the town,
Our toast is white, our ale is brown,
Our bowl it is made of the maple tree,
We be good fellows all, I drink to thee.

The mummers also perform outside Dursley church on the Sunday afternoon before Christmas (though check before travelling any great distance). The play originally featured St. George and the Dragon; the latter became the Turk at the time of the Crusades; then King George took over the saint's role, and the devil became 'Boneypart'. A characterisation of a local doctor is always included, and the play calls for lots of fighting. A 'Broad' is included in the Waterley Bottom version, a figure in a white sheet with a cow's skull head who drifts mainly around the crowd trying to frighten the children.

On Twelfth Night in Gloucestershire the custom of lighting thirteen Apostle fires and stamping out the one representing Judas continued until the beginning of this century; round the warmth of the rest of the fires plum cake and gingerbread husbands were eaten. Ginger, perhaps brought home by 'East India plunderers', was a common local ingredient. Gingerbread was popular in the area, and gingerbread husbands, 'men-shaped' biscuits, were being sold at many of the country fairs. **Mrs. Gurney's Gingersnaps** is an old country recipe: you need one cup sugar, one cup golden syrup, one cup melted butter (or a mixture of butter and lard), two teaspoons ground ginger, one teaspoon bicarbonate of soda dissolved in two tablespoons of hot water, and flour.

Work into the mixed ingredients enough flour to produce a stiff dough. Roll out as thin as possible on a floured board. Cut into small rounds and bake on a greased baking sheet in a moderate oven, 350 °F, gas mark 4, until browned.

A Gloucestershire Wassail

ANON

A version of the song referred to in Carol Wright's recipe
for Wassail Cup was printed in Gloucestershire Notes
And Queries *in 1902. It was quoted from an earlier*
book, John Brand's Observations On Popular Anti-
quities, *in which wassailing was associated with New*
Year's Eve. Since 'wassail' translates as 'be of good cheer'
the custom was in fact popular throughout the Twelve
Days, with Twelfth Night and Old Christmas Eve —
January 5 — favoured in some communities.

This song has since spread well beyond the county
boundaries, and is probably known as a choral piece today
throughout the English-speaking world. I was certainly
well familiar with something very close to it as a child in
the North of England. Dobbin and Captain in verses two
and three are horses, while Filpail is a cow; substitute
your favourite dog, cat or gerbil as you see fit. A version in
Minchinhampton went through various parts of the
'maister's' anatomy, right ear — barrel of good beer, right
arm — good crop of corn being among the more repeatable
rhymes.

Wassail, Wassail, all over the town
Our toast it is white, our ale it is brown;
Our bowl it is made of a maplin tree
We be good fellows all; I drink to thee.

Here's to Dobbin, and to his right ear,
God send our maister a happy New Year;
A happy New Year as e'er he did see —
With my Wassailing Bowl I drink to thee.

Here's to Captain, and to his right eye,
God send our mistress a good Christmas pye;
A good Christmas pye as e'er she did see —
With my Wassailing Bowl I drink to thee.

Here's to Filpail, and to her long tail,
God send our maister us never may fail
Of a cup of good beer, I pray you draw near,
And then you shall hear our jolly Wassail.

Be here any maids, I suppose here be some;
Sure they will not let young men stand on the cold stone,
Sing hey O maids, come trole back the pin,
And the fairest maid in the house, let us all in.

Come butler, come bring us a bowl of your best,
I hope your soul in Heaven may rest.
But if you do bring us a bowl of the small,
Then down fall butler, bowl, and all.

Edward II's Last Journey

I see no reason to put anyone off Christmas dinner by delving too graphically into the death of Edward II at Berkeley Castle in September 1327, but the journey his remains made up country to Gloucester in the depths of the December of that year had repercussions on the landscape still apparent from long stretches of the Cotswold edge today, for it paved the way for the magnificent rebuilding of the Cathedral.

After his overthrow by Queen Isabella, Prince Edward and Mortimer, Edward was imprisoned in Bristol until the discovery of a plot to rescue him prompted his captors to carry him north to Berkeley on Palm Sunday, 5 April. There his gaolers were the evil Maltravers and Gournay – the role of Lord Thomas Berkeley is very much in doubt – and the room where he met his death can still be seen in the castle.

He was not consigned to the dungeon but to a small chamber above it, where it was hoped that he would suffocate from the stench of rotting animal carcasses in the pit below. When he failed to succumb to this treatment Maltravers and Gournay murdered him in his bed and his screams of agony, ringing out over the rooftops of Berkeley to awake the sleeping townspeople, remain a chilling footnote of local folklore.

Not very Christmassy, any of this. But after that night of 22 September the question of Edward II's burial soon became paramount, and fear of offending Isabella and the barons led the abbots of St. Augustine in Bristol, Malmesbury and Kingswood, near Wotton-under-Edge, to refuse to perform the ceremony.

The man who eventually took the responsibility was Abbot

Edward II's fine effigy in Gloucester Cathedral, its dignity
intact through centuries-old graffiti.

John Thokey of Gloucester. A few days before Christmas he
sent an escort to bear the body from Berkeley in his own
carriage, and his monks received the king with great dignity
and ceremony before burying him close to the high altar.

There is no reason to think that Thokey was acting through
anything other than brave Christian motives; after all, the
negative response of his three neighbouring abbots could
scarcely have built up his expectations of any great good
coming from the gesture. But public opinion is a fickle thing.
It was not long before news of Edward's horrible death spread
far and wide, the boy king Edward III and the barons who
pulled his strings were at least as poor at ruling the country as
their predecessor, and before Thokey knew it Gloucester, with
the tomb, was a major place of pilgrimage.

With pilgrims came money – huge amounts of it – and eventually Edward III himself was granting privileges to the abbey. The result was a massive rebuilding programme, and much of what we now know as Gloucester Cathedral dates from the years immediately following Edward's burial. The south transept, the choir, the north transept, the great east window: all followed in the fourteenth century, and Gloucester led the way in establishing the Perpendicular style that was to dominate English Gothic architecture for the next 150 years.

The late David Verey was just one historian who was happy to credit Thokey's bravery after Edward's death for this stylistic breakthrough. And since pilgrims were still rolling up more than a century later, it is not too fanciful to add Gloucester's fine New Inn of *c.* 1457 to the list of consequences of Christmas 1327 which are still in evidence today.

from

A Cotswold Village

J. ARTHUR GIBBS

Published in the final years of the last century, A
Cotswold Village *did much to popularise this part of the
country in general and the area around Bibury in
particular. Gibbs, a product of Eton and Oxford, settled
in Ablington and wrote about the hamlet and its
characters in a way that runs the risk of sounding
patronising today, but which at the time was a model of
gentlemanly liberality.*

*Perhaps it is not too cynical to suggest that at least some
of the volume's early success could be put down to the
author's death, at the age of thirty-one, within a couple of
years of its publication; tragedy has sold wares before and
since then, and from the third edition onwards the book
was prefaced by a touching eulogy written by a close
relative.*

It is Christmas Day, and so lovely is the weather that I am
sitting on the terrace watching the warm, grateful sun
gradually disappearing through the grey ash trunks in the
hanging wood beyond the river. The birds are singing with all
the promise of an early spring. There is scarcely a breath of
wind stirring, and one might almost imagine it to be April.

Tom Peregrine, clad in his best Sunday homespun, passes along his well-worn track through the rough grass beyond the water, intent on visiting his vermin traps, or bent on some form of destruction, for he is never happy unless he is killing. My old friend the one-legged cock pheasant, who for the third year in succession has contrived to escape our annual battue, comes up to my feet and takes the bread I offer.

When he was flushed by the beaters there was no need to call 'Spare him', for with all the cunning of a veteran he towered straight into the skies and passed over the guns out of shot. Two fantail pigeons of purest white, sitting in a dark yew tree that overhangs the stream a hundred yards away, make the prettiest picture in the world against the dusky foliage.

Splash! A great brown trout rolls in the shallow water like a porpoise in the sea. A two-pounder in this little stream makes as much fuss as a twenty-pound salmon in the mighty Tweed.

Hark! Was that a lamb bleating down in old Mr. Peregrine's meadow? It was: the first lamb, herald of the spring that is to be. May its little life be as peaceful as this its first birthday: less stormy than the life of the Lamb whose birth all people celebrate today.

The rooks are cawing, and a faint cry of plover comes from the hill.

Soft and grey is the winter sky, but behold! Round the sun in the west there arises a perfect solar halo, very similar to an ordinary rainbow, but smaller in its arc and fainter in its hues of yellow and rose – a very beautiful phenomenon, and one seldom to be seen in England. Halos of this nature are supposed to arise from the double refraction of the rays from the sun as the light passes through thin clouds, or from the transmission of light through particles of ice. It lingers a full quarter of an hour, and then dies away. Does this bode rough weather? Surely the cruel Boreas and the frost will not come suddenly on us after this lovely, mild Christmas?

Listen to the Christmas bells ringing two miles away at Barnsley village! We can never tire of the sound here, for it is only on very still days that it reaches us across the wolds.

> Hark! In the air, around, above,
>> The angelic music soars and swells,
> And in the garden that I love
>> I hear the sound of Christmas bells.

> Peace and goodwill 'twixt rich and poor!
>> Goodwill and peace 'twixt class and class!
> Let old with new, let Prince with boor
>> Send round the bowl, and drain the glass.
>> **Alfred Austin**

I have culled these lines from the poet laureate's charming *Christmas Carol,* as they are both singularly beautiful and singularly appropriate to our Cotswold village. I take the liberty of saying that in our little hamlet there *is* peace and goodwill 'twixt rich and poor at Christmas-time.

Our humble rejoicings during this last Christmas were very similar to those of a hundred years ago. They included a grand smoking concert at the club, during which the mummers gave an admirable performance of their old play, of which more anon; then a big feed for every man, woman and child of the hamlet, about a hundred souls, was held in the manor house; added to which we received visits from carol singers and musicians of all kinds to the number of seventy-two, reckoning up the total aggregate of the different bands, all of whom were welcomed, for Christmas comes but once a year, after all, and 'the more the merrier' should be our motto at this time.

So from villages three or four miles away came bands of children to sing the old, old songs. The brass band, including old grey-haired men who fifty years ago with strings and

woodwind led the psalmody at Chedworth Church, come too, and play inside the hall. We do not brew at home nowadays. Even such old-fashioned Conservatives as old Mr. Peregrine senior have at length given up the custom, so we cannot, like Sir Roger, allow a greater quantity of malt to our small beer at Christmas; but we take good care to order in some four or five eighteen-gallon casks at this time. Let it be added that we never saw any man the worse for drink in consequence of this apparent indiscretion. But then, we have a butler of the old school.

When we held our Yuletide revels in the manor house, and the old walls rang with the laughter and merriment of the whole hamlet, for farmers as well as labourers honoured us, it occurred to me that the bigotphones, which had been lying by in a cupboard for about a twelvemonth, might amuse the company. Bigotphones, I must explain to those readers who are uninitiated, are delightfully simple contrivances fitted

A winter's afternoon in Avening.

with reed mouthpieces – exact representations in mockery of the various instruments that make up a brass band – but composed of strong cardboard, and dependent solely on the judicious application of the human lips and the skilful modulation of the human voice for their effect.

These being produced, an impromptu band was formed: young Peregrine seized the bassoon, the carter took the clarionet [sic], the shepherd the French horn, the cowman the trombone, and, seated at the piano, I myself conducted the orchestra. Never before have I been so astonished as I was by the unexpected musical ability displayed. No matter what tune I struck up, that heterogeneous orchestra played it as if they had been doing nothing else all their lives. *The British Grenadiers, The Eton Boating Song, Two Lovely Black Eyes* (solo, young Peregrine on the bassoon) *A Fine Hunting Day* – all and sundry were performed in perfect time and without a false note. Singularly enough, it is very difficult for the voice to 'go flat' on the bigotphone.

Then, not content with these popular songs, we inaugurated a dance. Now could be seen the beautiful and accomplished Miss Peregrine doing the light fantastic round the stone floor of the hall to the tune of *See Me Dance The Polka;* then, too, the stately Mrs. Peregrine insisted on our playing *Sir Roger de Coverley,* and it was danced with that pomp and ceremony which such occasions alone are wont to show. None of your 'kitchen lancers' for us hamlet folk; we leave that kind of thing to the swells and nobs.

Tom Peregrine alone was baffled. Whilst his family in general were bowing there, curtseying here, clapping hands and passing under to the right in the usual Sir Roger style, he stood in grey homespun of the best material – I never yet saw a Cotswold man in a vulgar chessboard suit – and as he stood he marvelled greatly, exclaiming now and then: 'Well, I never; this is something new, to be sure! I never saw such things in all my life, never!' He would not dance; but seizing one of the bigotphones, he blew into it until I was in some anxiety lest he should have an apoplectic fit. I need scarcely say he failed to produce a single note.

Thus our Yuletide festivities passed away, all enjoying themselves immensely, and thus was sealed the bond of goodwill 'twixt class and class for the coming year.

Whilst the younger folks danced, the fathers of the hamlet walked on tiptoe with fearful tread around the house, looking at the faded family portraits. I was pleased to find that what they liked best was the ancient armour; for, said they, 'Doubtless squire wore that in the old battles hereabouts, when Oliver Cromwell was round these parts.' On my pointing out the picture of the man who built the house three hundred years ago, they surrounded it and gazed at the features for a great length of time; indeed, I feared that they would never come away, so fascinated were they by this relic of antiquity, illustrating the ancient though simple annals of their village.

I persuaded the head of our mummer troop to write out their play as it was handed down to him by his predecessors. This he did in a fine bold hand on four sides of foolscap. Unfortunately the literary quality of the lines is so poor that they are hardly worth reproducing, except as a specimen of the poetry of very early times handed down by oral tradition. Suffice it to say that the *dramatis personae* are five in number – viz. Father Christmas, Saint George, a Turkish Knight, a Doctor and an Old Woman. All are dressed in paper flimsies of various shapes and colours. First of all enters Father Christmas.

> 'In comes I old Father Christmas,
> Welcome in or welcome not,
> Sometimes cold and sometimes hot.
> I hope Father Christmas will never be forgot.'

Harsh weather for shopping in Minchinhampton.

Then Saint George comes in, and after a great deal of bragging he fights the 'most dreadful battle that ever was known', his adversary being the knight 'just come from Turkey-land', with the inevitable result that the Turkish knight falls. This brings in the Doctor, who suggests the following remedies:

> 'Give him a bucket of dry hot ashes to eat,
> Groom him down with a bezom stick,
> And give him a yard and a half of pump water to drink.'

For these offices he mentions that his fee is fifty guineas, but he will take ten pounds, adding:

> 'I can cure the itchy pitchy,
> Palsy, and the gout;
> Pains within or pains without;
> A broken leg or a broken arm,
> Or a broken limb of any sort.
> I cured old Mother Roundabout. . .'

He declares that he is not one of those 'quack doctors who

97

go about from house to house telling you more lies in one half-hour than what you can find true in seven years.'

So the knight just come from Turkey-land is resuscitated and sent back to his own country.

Last of all the old woman speaks:

'In comes I old Betsy Bub;
On my shoulder I carry my tub,
And in my hand a dripping-pan.
Don't you think I'm a jolly old man?

Now last Christmas my father killed a fat hog,
And my mother made black-puddings enough to choke a
                                                    dog,
And they hung them up with a pudden string
Till the fat dropped out and the maggots crawled in. . .'

The mummers' play, of which the above is a very brief summary, lasts about half an hour and includes many songs of a topical nature.

Yes, Christmas is Christmas still in the heart of old England. We are apt to talk of the good old days that are no more, lamenting the customs and country sports that have passed away; but let us not forget that two hundred years hence, when we who are living now will have long passed 'that bourne from which no traveller returns', our descendants, as they sit round their hearths at Yuletide, may in the same way regret the grand old times when good Victoria – the greatest monarch of all ages – was Queen of England.

The Oxen

THOMAS HARDY

Hardy was seventy-five when he wrote this poem in 1915, his career as a novelist long past, and the combination of his advancing years and the backdrop of the First World War add poignancy to this simple childhood tale of lost innocence. Based on the old legend that farm animals bow down as if in prayer at midnight on Christmas Eve, recalling the oxen and asses of Bethlehem, it seems to me the most touching and deeply-felt of all our Christmas poems. And while the Cotswolds cannot truly lay claim to the poet, all of us who know the hills have our own ideas of where the lonely barton by yonder coomb might be; there is one near Bisley, happily still not converted into a five-bedroom, three-bathroom des. res., that never fails to put me in mind of Hardy's haunting words.

Christmas Eve, and twelve of the clock.
'Now they are all on their knees,'
An elder said as we sat in a flock
By the embers in hearthside ease.

We pictured the meek mild creatures where
They dwelt in their strawy pen,
Nor did it occur to one of us there
To doubt they were kneeling then.

So fair a fancy few would weave
In these years! Yet, I feel,
If someone said on Christmas Eve,
'Come; see the oxen kneel

In the lonely barton by yonder coomb
Our childhood used to know,'
I should go with him in the gloom,
Hoping it might be so.

from

Rural Rides of the Bristol Churchgoer

JOSEPH LEECH

As a Rural Rider Leech was a little way behind William Cobbett, whose wide-ranging travels were published in book form in 1830. But at his best he had something of the old radical's spleenful turn of phrase, and he was certainly at the top of his form when he chronicled the Christmas morning procession in Thornbury in 1844. In spite of the scorn he poured on the ceremony, the practice of parading the often infirm poor of the town continued for decades after his visit.

The Thornbury Christmas procession outside the Swan in the late nineteenth century, little changed from the scene Leech derided in the 1840s.

Were I not in a hurry I should have been disposed to loiter on Almondsbury Hill, which overlooks so noble a prospect, with the broad waters of the Severn bounding the view; but the bells beginning to ring in the old and picturesque little church, with its lead-covered spire in the hollow, told me I had no time to lose, so I pushed on without pause to the Ship at Alveston.

Here, for the first time, I got a peep of the fair church tower of Thornbury with its beautiful balustraded top, but as I looked down on the 'old burgh' with its old houses snugly nestling amongst old trees, no sound reached me, no bells boomed out their Christmas peals, and I began to think I had arrived too late, not only for the procession, but prayers. What, thought I, after riding twelve miles to see them, have they presumed to march to church without my being there to see? I pushed John to a more energetic walk than usual, and as I pulled up at the Swan porch the first question I asked of my landlady, who promptly made her appearance, was if prayers had commenced.

'No, Sir,' said she. 'They do not commence today until half past eleven, on account of the Mayor; the usual time is eleven.'

It appears that Thornbury (proud place) has a Mayor and Corporation, and the principal and only duty which the great civic functionary has to perform during his year of office is to provide coffee for his co-councilmen and the incumbent of the parish at his residence on Christmas morning – and having discussed that, and a quantity of hot rolls, to walk, preceded by some poor men and women, through the town to church.

In consideration of the Mocha and munchets the service is accordingly delayed, as we have already seen, half an hour. It never struck their worships – it never occurred to the incumbent – that by beginning their breakfast 30 minutes sooner, the parishioners who have not the good fortune to partake of cake and coffee at the Mayor's expense need not be obliged to postpone their dinners half an hour, to say nothing of the very secondary position in which it places the celebration of the solemn service of the church.

But it was more than half an hour, for I stood with my back against the wooden column of the Swan porch, still waiting the apparition of the civic procession, some minutes after the hands of the Town Hall clock pointed to half past eleven; and I began to think that his worship had added a *demitasse* of ratafie (fruit liqueur) to his *dejeuner* when a person who happened to come up at the time, and of whom I made some enquiries, assured me this could not be the case, as the Mayor was an impregnable teetotaller.

At length a rush of little boys with red noses announced that a movement of that momentous body, the Mayor and Corporation of Thornbury, had taken place, and that the functionaries had really finished their breakfast. First came a file of old women in gowns, aprons and bonnets alike, then a string of elderly men in brown coats with very bright buttons – the Corporation of Thornbury wish their good deeds to *shine* before men – and black hats with very broad brims, the gift of the Corporation, the recipients being left to find inexpressibles for themselves.

The ancient Romans showed their glory by the line of captives that followed their cavalcades; the Corporation of Thornbury display their charity by the number of paupers that precede their procession. They are not the people, bless their hearts, to 'do good by stealth and blush to find it fame'. People may call your worships 'Pharisaical functionaries', but depend upon it, there's nothing like letting all the world know your benevolence: once commence the silent system of almsgiving, and half the close-fisted in the country will take credit to themselves for the acts of charity done by others in secret, and the public will be cheated out of its compassion by swindlers. The poor passed, two tall staff-men swaggered on in front of the party, and then came the Mayor, in a broad-brimmed hat and black surtout and a brown cotton umbrella, having the Rev. Townsend Stephens, canonically clad, on his right, and a detachment of brother aldermen filling up the rear. They were a good-humoured, good-natured, good-looking set of gentlemen, and as they wiped their mouths after the Mayor's muffins, none could seem more happy or contented. But they were piteously shorn of their pomp – no state carriage, no gold chain and silver gown, no insignia or precious metal, unless, indeed, a decent-sized silver mace – I forgot the mace – and a white wand which I also neglected to enumerate.

I don't know what there was remarkable or worthy of remark in my contour or brown coat, but as the procession passed the Swan they all, including his Worship and his Reverence, stared at me as if I had two heads, and there was a whispering and seeming consultation amongst them, which I fondly put down for a friendly contest between the Mayor and the Rev. Townsend Stephens as to which should have the pleasure of asking me that day to dinner. Here, however, I was mistaken. . . .

I followed the procession, and had the inexpressible delight of hearing two fellows in fustian jackets – I pledge my word for the fact – exclaim as they crushed by me in the crowd: 'The Church-Goer is in town.' Talk of celebrity; that's what I call glory, to find that one's reputation, one's title and likeness had travelled twelve miles from Bristol, and that the very bumpkins in the street syllabled my name.

My moral reflections brought me and the procession to the churchyard, and I leaned over the wall to look at the little cortege as it wound up the gravel walk. There was one poor man amongst the recipients of the brown coats who had some affliction of the legs, and as he toiled along, a prominent and somewhat painful object in the affair, I felt disposed to regret that the civic body should have thought it necessary for their pity-moving purposes to exhibit him in the procession.

from

The Glorious Glosters

TIM CAREW

The most significant chapter in the recent history of the Gloucestershire Regiment was the Korean war of the early 1950s, and in particular the Glosters' heroic role in the Battle of Imjin River in April, 1951. This excerpt from Tim Carew's regimental history takes us back to the uneasy Christmas of 1950, when old sweats and National Service youngsters alike made the best of the situation as only soldiers can.

On 16 December the Glosters took up new positions about seven miles north of Seoul, the capital of South Korea, to await the oncoming Chinese. Their defensive positions spread along a valley bounded by towering hills, running off from the main supply route to the north. This became known to the Battalion as Compo Valley, after the composite rations which were brought up each day from the railhead. It was frugal fare indeed, and consisted of stringy bacon, the ubiquitous bully beef, soya sausages, tinned steak and kidney pudding – all pudding and no steak and kidney, as one frustrated gourmand described it – dehydrated potatoes, and very little else.

The (vastly experienced) 29th Brigade were now in Corps
Reserve, and in the Glosters tension lessened appreciably. The
new area seemed to offer some prospect of near-permanency
and the Battalion, taking the viewpoint that any fool can be
uncomfortable, set about making themselves a new home. The
result was universally known as Shanty Town, a diverse
collection of huts and holes constructed from corrugated iron.
Weird and wonderful dwellings sprang up, and in spite of the
appalling weather the Battalion settled down to a fairly
comfortable life by Korean war standards; there were naked
lights showing in the darkness, baths and cinema shows.
Dining halls appeared as if by magic, petrol drums mysteriously disappeared, only to reappear as ovens, and a huge stack
of mail, the second since the Battalion landed at Pusan, put in
a welcome appearance.

Suddenly it was Christmas Eve, 1950.

Reports had been received of a massive Chinese build-up on
the Imjin River. Anticipating a possible enemy attack in
strength on Christmas Day, Brigadier Brodie ordered that
Christmas should be celebrated on 24 December. As a result of
near-miracles of improvisation, the Battalion celebrated
Christmas in almost traditional style, in a blinding snow-
storm. Leaving the minimum number of sentries to guard
against Chinese interruption, the Glosters trooped down from
the icy mountains and filled their mess-tins with turkey,
carved by officers with bayonets.

The principal architect of the Battalion's Christmas dinner
was Corporal Taffy Watkins. In fifteen years of army cookery
he had cooked Christmas dinners on the North-west Frontier
of India, in North Africa and Italy; in Korea he showed a
staunch determination to be undeterred by the elements.
Turkeys frozen solid on arrival were thawed out and roasted in
improvised petrol-drum ovens. There was roast turkey in
sufficient portions to satisfy any Briton, but the trimmings

were distinctly American – celery dressing, giblet gravy, snowflake and candied sweet potatoes, cranberry sauce and whole-kernel corn.

There was no shortage of liquor and B Company, in particular, showed considerable enterprise. With memories of inventive wassailing in Jamaica to guide them, Lieutenant Norrish and Sergeant Claxton produced a cocktail of startling potency from a well-tried Caribbean recipe – a mixture of gin, whisky, rum, American issue orange juice, American fruit cocktail, local hooch and evaporated milk.

Two pianos were perched on the side of a hill – battered and mildewed instruments with many notes missing. Carols were sung and company comedians did impersonations of sergeant-majors. Climatically, it was as hard and rough a Christmas as the British Army in the field had ever experienced, but the Glosters did their best with it and emerged undoubted victors over the gross elements.

Christmas Day was quiet, as were the days following it, but the peaceful lull was short-lived. Early on the morning of 1 January 1951 the Chinese Communist forces crossed the Imjin River and fell upon the 1st Republic of Korea Infantry Division.

The Battalion, as Corps Reserve, was alerted at 0545 hours. By 1000 hours they had moved forward, been halted, turned about and switched to a new area. Colonel Carne tramped the hills ahead, laying out yet another defensive position, into which the Battalion moved at nightfall. It seemed certain that at long last the Glosters would now see action, and just before dawn on 3 January came the first real fight between the enemy and the 29th Brigade.

As Hard As Winking

HUMPHREY PHELPS

Christmas comes but once a year – but commercial Christmas comes earlier year by year. Before the leaves of autumn have finished falling those asinine TV jingles assault the ear and insult the senses. Then the shops sprout synthetic holly and frost, the streets are crowded and the cash registers jangle, for it seems that everybody but me can find just the right things to buy for presents. I like Christmas by about four o'clock on Christmas Eve, but how I hate the weeks preceding it, except when I am in the fields.

Christmas comes sooner to all of us as we grow older, and with age come memories. I can still recall the thrill of finding the filled stocking, and Christmas – indeed, life itself – was not the same when Father Christmas no longer visited me.

Then there were the parties. The teas always started with bread and butter and jelly, which I disliked, but even more I loathed the games: musical chairs, postman's knock, and worst of all the one in which you had to wink. I was unable to wink, and unable to be jolly to order, for that matter. They are two disabilities I have never outgrown.

Even now, if I go to a party, I invariably find myself alone and silent in a corner while all around I see people laughing and talking. There must be something the matter with you, I tell myself, yet normally I am garrulous, or so I am told.

Christmas morning forty years ago, early 1940s, just left school, sitting on a three-legged stool, bucket clasped between the knees, head thrust into warm flank of cow. 'Ping' went the first drawn milk as it hit the bottom of the bucket, and later, as it began to fill, the sound changed to a gentle 'fuzz-fuzz'. There were other sounds in that lantern-lit shed; the jingle of the chains around the cows' necks, the rustle of straw beneath their feet and their steady munching. The air was redolent of cows and the pulped swedes they were eating.

We pulped those swedes by hand, turning a handle round and round; they were hard to pulp, too, much harder than mangolds, which were never used until after Christmas. After milking there were more swedes to pulp for the bullocks in the yard. Never mind how cold the morning; ten or twenty minutes on the pulper acted as a wonderful warmer.

The pulped swedes were carried in a large oval basket to the yards where the fat bullocks stood waiting, pumping from their nostrils twin jets of breath in the cold air. All their drinking water had to be carried in buckets, and on frosty days they always seemed thirstier. Carrying water was a slow, laborious job, and with each successive journey our hands grew colder. Cutting hay out of the rick with the big salmon-shaped knife was a pleasant task, however; the cut hay smelled of summer and I felt it retained its warmth, too.

There were so many handles in those days, pulper handles, milk- and water-bucket handles, hay-knife handles, pike and fork handles and shovel handles. A handle for almost every job, and every job done by hand. Now I wonder how we did it. Today all that hand work would be accounted drudgery; perhaps it was, but to most of the work then – except water-carrying – there was a rhythm. Usually there was company, too, and we laughed and talked as we worked.

Ten, twelve, fourteen years on; the morning air at Christmas was redolent of silage instead of swedes. A milking

machine had replaced the bucket and stool, neither cows nor bullocks had horns, and a pocket-knife had replaced the hay-knife because hay was tied up in parcels; but water still had to be carried by hand – and Father Christmas was calling again. I relived the same old thrill as my children shouted with delight at the feel of filled stockings.

And so on to the 1980s; the Christmas morning air will still be redolent of silage, but water no longer has to be carried. Milking done, cattle fed, breakfast eaten, logs on the fire; this, as Mr. Pickwick observed, is real comfort, as I sit and wait for the arrival of my grandchildren. Indeed, it is more than comfort, it is pure delight, for Father Christmas is alive and well again.

The Real Tailor of Gloucester

The image of Simpkin the cat wandering in the Christmas snow in College Court is one of the most appealing and abiding memories of Beatrix Potter's classic children's book *The Tailor of Gloucester,* which has been a million-seller twice over since its first publication in December, 1902.

Even those who have not read the book know how the Tailor of Gloucester fell ill while making an embroidered suit in which the Mayor was to be married on Christmas Day in the

The Tailor of Gloucester's shop in College Court.

The interior of the Tailor's shop, modelled closely on the
drawings in Beatrix Potter's book.

morning – and how the mice worked through the night to finish it for him, all but a buttonhole on the satin waistcoat which they left undone with the message 'NO MORE TWIST' attached in 'little teeny weeny writing'.

The story behind Beatrix Potter's tale began in 1894, when she first visited her cousin Caroline Hutton at Harescombe Grange, near Stroud. Aged twenty-seven, Beatrix had led a very sheltered life with her parents in London and her first book was still seven years away, but she was already an avid observer and sketcher, and one story told by a lady taking tea at the grange caught her imagination in particular.

The visitor told of John Samuel Prichard (d. 1934), who had displayed a notice in his window to the effect of: 'Have your suit made here, where the work is done at night by fairies'. Unlike Potter's creation, Prichard was a young and respected tailor rushed off his feet with orders, and he grew increasingly depressed when it became obvious that he was not going to finish a waistcoat commissioned for the new mayor to wear at the procession for the opening of the annual root, fruit and grain show, still a fixture on the local calendar.

On the Saturday before the show he was so sick and dejected that he closed up early and went home; and on the Monday morning when he opened up, there, sure enough, was the waistcoat with the message NO MORE TWIST.

Beatrix Potter went about her task with a will, and with complete professionalism. She sketched the shop exterior in College Court when she visited Gloucester a few days later, drew several interiors of old cottages in the Stroud area as guides for her indoor scenes, and put in hours of further research at a tailor's shop close to her home in Chelsea. Before she published the book – which was first written as a gift for a friend's little daughter, Freda Moore, for Christmas, 1901 – she told John Prichard of her plans, and assured him she would depict the tailor as an old man.

It was not until 1979 that Prichard's son Douglas, about to retire from his air travel business in Bahrain, told Beatrix Potter's biographer Margaret Lane the full story. Some of the tailor's assistants had taken refuge in the shop on the Saturday night after a drinking bout, and the next morning, rather than revealing themselves in their unshaven state to the cathedral-goers in their Sunday best, they stayed in the shop until darkness fell. Needless to say, there was nothing to do but work – and that they did until there was literally no more twist. So far as their boss was concerned, however, they were quite content to credit the good deed to the fairies, rather than confess that they had been drunk and owned a key to the premises.

The final twist, to coin a phrase, came at around the time of Douglas Prichard's revelation, when the publishers Frederick Warne, after failing on a previous occasion, acquired the College Court shop from a long-established antique dealer and transformed it into a Tailor of Gloucester's shop and museum which, both inside and out, echoes Beatrix Potter's drawings with pleasing accuracy. It completed yet another chapter in a story in which fact and fiction are confusingly entwined.

Christmas with
the Mitfords

DIANA ALEXANDER

*The 'Mitford girls' were the talk of London society — and
the popular press that glamorized it — in the inter-war
years, and later Nancy and Jessica recorded their
experiences in a number of successful books. The other sisters
were Diana, who married Oswald Mosley, Unity, an
admirer of Hitler, Deborah, who became Duchess of
Devonshire — and 'the quiet one', Pam, who as the Hon.
Mrs. Jackson lived in an upland village near Cheltenham
until her death in the early 1990s.*

It was not until the revival of interest in the family in recent
times that the media discovered Pam, the quiet, shy sister, a
countrywoman and superb cook, who recently celebrated her
eightieth birthday at home in the Cotswolds. But she was
always blessed with a youthful sense of fun, and the years have
not diminished it as she reminisces about family Christmases
of long ago as if they were last year.

By the time all the girls and their brother Tom were
growing up the family had moved from Batsford Park, near
Moreton-in-Marsh, to an East Cotswold estate at Swinbrook,
Oxfordshire. Pam recalls that her mother, Lady Redesdale,
started shopping for Christmas in October, and this meant
several trips to Oxford — never London — to buy presents for

The Mitfords' Christmas fancy dress in 1925. In the back row
Diana is under the sheet, Nancy is the tramp and Pam is third
from right, having avoided dressing up. Front: Unity is on the
left, Jessica is in the beard next to her, and Deborah is on the
right.

the tree from Elliston and Cavell and the children's favourite,
Hooton's Bazaar.

By the end of November they began to pack the parcels, a
mammoth task since there was a present for every adult who
worked on the estate and a toy and a garment for each of the
workers' children. Many of the clothes had been knitted by
Lady Redesdale earlier in the year.

On Christmas Eve a huge tree from the estate was brought
in and decorated by the family, and then all the uncles, aunts
and cousins arrived amid great excitement. Next was the tea
party for a hundred guests from the estate. First came the food
to quieten excited children, and then the arrival of Father
Christmas to the sound of 'sleigh bells'.

His lordship would fling open the door to admit the
scarlet-clad figure with his sack bulging with presents. The

parson, Mr. Foster, always came late to the party, some time after Father Christmas had departed, and it was years before the Mitford children solved that puzzle. . . .

After tea there were party games with music provided by Lady Redesdale at the piano, and at 7 o'clock all the guests went home, each child carrying an orange and a bag of sweets. It was Pam's job to wrap the sweets in home-made bags, and she always wished she could eat them all herself.

The whole household cleared the remains of the party, and there was scarcely time for a quick cold supper before the carol singers arrived from the village, to be invited in for a glass of beer or cider served by Lord Redesdale from large barrels.

After this it was time to hang up the Christmas stockings, which the children did until they were almost grown up. The excitement was even more intense at 5.30 on Christmas morning, when they were opened. Each stocking had an orange in the toe and envelopes from the aunts and uncles, usually containing 10s. or £1; one red-letter Christmas Day one of Pam's envelopes had a £5 note in it. . . .

Soon after breakfast the family would walk to morning service at Swinbrook Church, which was decorated with holly and chrysanthemums. Mr. Foster always chose the children's favourite carols and made the service fairly short, as he knew everyone was anxious to get home for turkey and plum pudding. A walk was always necessary after lunch to make room for the Christmas cake; and then came the Dressing Up.

The children vanished to the attic to look in the dressing-up box, full of fancy dress costumes and some of Lady Redesdale's old evening dresses. The costumes were supposed to be a secret, but as everyone knew what was in the box there were seldom many surprises. One year Nancy, an expert in these matters, pulled off a rare coup by disappearing when dinner was served, only to emerge as an Egyptian mummy from a hinged window seat as the guests were leaving the dining room.

The Hon. Mrs. Pamela Jackson in her later years.

Lord Redesdale's costume never varied – he always wore a dressing gown and a 'ghastly red wig'. Pam admits that she was very bad at the game and always appeared as Lady Rowena from *Ivanhoe*; her dress was a long piece of red crinkled *crêpe-de-chine* with a hole for her head, the neck was trimmed with golden wooden beads, and a belt completed the vision. The long gown meant she could keep on her long woolly underwear, no small consideration in the country houses of sixty years ago, but Nancy would never let her get away with it, pulling up the skirt to reveal her sister's knee-length bloomers to the world!

When supper was cleared the house party reassembled around the dining table – a copy of the one in Leonardo's *The Last Supper* – and played a game called Commerce, for which Lord Redesdale produced money prizes ranging from 10s. to 1d. 'The Game' often went on until 11.30, by which time the adults were wilting visibly while the children grew more and more boisterous. The 'babies', Unity, Jessica and Deborah, had long since been taken off to the nursery.

After all the excitement, on Boxing Day there was the gloomy thought that all the guests would be going home tomorrow, and life would return to normal. The children always longed for deep snow so that the uncles and aunts could not reach the station – a five-mile drive by pony and trap when the weather was too bad for the car. Pam remembers this happening only twice, and feels that the adults may not have been so ecstatic as the children at finding their escape to London closed.

The festivities were not yet over, however, for on New Year's Eve the mummers arrived and performed their traditional play, with St. George, the Dragon, the Turkish Knight and the village children reciting their parts in a monotone. It was in this group that a youthful Bob Arnold – Tom Forrest in *The Archers* – began his acting career.

All too soon after this came Twelfth Night, when the tree was dismantled and the decorations, the fairy doll, the tinsel and the clip-on candle holders were put away for another year. So, too, were the sponge and water bucket Lord Redesdale always hid behind the tree as a fire precaution.

Pam loves recalling those Christmases of the 1920s, but she admits to enjoying herself just as much today – especially as she no longer has to endure that Simply Dreadful Dressing Up.

Christmas Letters from a Gloster

IVOR GURNEY

Ivor Gurney, the Gloucester poet and musician whose gassing during the First World War led to his death in a London mental hospital on Boxing Day, 1937, will forever be remembered as a tragic figure. Yet a collection of letters published under the title Stars in a Dark Night *in 1986 showed him to be a young man full of affection and fun, as well as one of massive artistic potential.*

The letters were written to members of the Chapman family of High Wycombe, with whom he was close both before and after the war, when he was a church organist in the town. They welcomed him like a returning son when he was fit enough to resume his musical studies in 1919 – but very soon afterwards, it was their unhappy lot to discover that their beloved Ivor would never be the same again.

Chelmsford, December 1915
My Dear Old Winnie,

I am sorry you have been sick and at such an untactful time of holidays. Perhaps it is all better now. Bless you my child, I hope so. As for the photo, it simply hasn't arrived, and my laziness has prevented me writing to know why.

I hope to see you next Sunday, and it is fairly certain that I shall – or on Saturday.

What a funny Xmas this will be! Away from everything in the way of Children and ping-pong. Anyway, I shall be feeling much better this year than last, and not such a drag on the entertainment as then; for we simply must get up some sort of entertainment in this dead-alive unfortunate hole. Either 4 or 8 of us are plotting how to make believe that army life may be made jolly about Christmas time. We'll do it, somehow. Unless they stick us on guard, or the extremely military operation of picking up paper. Anyway, I hope all you will concentrate all your phsycic [sic] faculties on having a damgood time then; and remembering me only to pledge me in the quaffing of huge tankards of beer, to the shouts of Waeshhael! Let the ancestral hall of St. Michael, and its stately keep and barbican echo to the sound.

Epic on the Celebration of the Mass of Christ

> Kinkering Kongs
> Do ping their pongs.
> And title-takers
> Get stomach-achers.

Tell tales all round again. Put your hand on each others backs, and count the shivers. Judge each ghost tale, not only by the frequency of the shivers but also by their duration and wobblyness.
Goodbye dear and best wishes
Yours affectionately
Ivor

France, January 1917
My Dear Old Win

Still here and not there, as is perhaps to be expected. No leave yet, that is to say; but who knows? I may arrive home from the office tonight and find a telegram 'Will you come and teach me how? Lloyd George' (reply half-prepaid). Or 'Do stop them, old man – Wilhelm' (not pre-paid) lying on the hall table. This might mean quite a few days in Blighty, in which case I shall hurry at once to St. Micks . . . and present my never-for-one-single-phsycological [sic] -moment-to-be-forgotten Winifred with the one souvenir I have – the tattered remains of a G. pocket book – if it lasts till then.

I hope Christmas went off all right and fine – that Daddy was not grumpy and La Comtesse grumpy at his grumpiness. I trust you danced the roundelay and Fa-la-la-ed to any extent. Stap me, had I been there, would not I have taken part in these innocent revels? Yea, by the to [sic] old Pig of Brixham, marry, so would I!

And how's Arthur and how's that little imp of restlessness Micky, the human Soap-Bubble? How many goals has Arthur the Hope of his Side managed to score?

I want to know all Mrs. It is port wine oatcakes and chews of bacca for me. Hogmanay was happy and rowdy just round here – happier than it was in Scotland, the men come back from leave say.

Well I hope High Wycombe put some go in the parting kick.

Good bye
Yours affectionately
Ivor

The Bishop's Christmas, 1289

DAVID ALDRED

I like to see Bishop Richard de Swinfield of Hereford as a medieval wholefood enthusiast; as David Aldred, a leading Gloucestershire local historian recalls, whole calves, whole pigs and whole fowl graced his table when he held his festivities near Cheltenham in 1289.

It was a combination of circumstances that forced the Bishop of Hereford to spend the Christmas of 1289 at his manor at Prestbury, near Cheltenham, rather than at his favourite retreat at Bosbury, near Ledbury. But records show that he was determined to make the best of a bad job with a feast of immense proportions.

Not a lot would tempt him from Bosbury at this time of year, but a summons to attend Parliament in the wake of Richard I's return to England after three years in France, and the Archbishop of Canterbury's simultaneous convention of a congregation of bishops in London, convinced him that he and his large household would have to spend the festive season *en route* at Prestbury.

We know of his visit through John de Kempsey, his chaplain, who supplemented his religious duties by keeping a meticulous record of the bishop's expenditure. From his terse financial statements in abbreviated Latin emerges a fascinating story, full of human interest, and it does not take much

An artist's impression of the bishop's feast.

imagination to recreate the kind of Christmas enjoyed by the privileged few in medieval times.

Richard de Swinfield, a native of Kent, succeeded his patron Thomas de Cantelupe as Bishop of Hereford in 1283. He was a good shepherd of his diocese and a generous patron of poor scholars, but he shunned even the life of quiet Hereford for the calm of his rural manors, particularly Bosbury. It was from there that he made his first preparations for Christmas by sending his servant Robert de Calewe to Prestbury to organise the burning of charcoal for the fires and the brewing of the festive beer. Thicker and sweeter than the modern drink, this special Christmas beer was made from a malt of wheat, oats and barley, and contained no hops; it was brewed late because it kept badly.

Robert returned on December 16, having spent nineteen

days at Prestbury; he was obviously kept very busy there, as the accounts record the purchase of candles and the payment of brew-wives – interestingly, the only reference to women in the whole account roll, since the bishop lived in an all-male household. Unlike the beer, the wine was brought in and sent with the furniture and baggage on the day Robert returned, to ensure its arrival in Prestbury well ahead of Richard.

Although the bishop and his entourage left on the following day, his was a leisurely progress, via Gloucester. We can imagine him on his new horse, purchased by Thomas the groom only three days before, for John de Kempsey kept close account of his master's clothing. He scarcely sounds as if he looked like a bishop: he wore a fur cap which had cost 3s. 1d., his underwear was of linen and wool and his supertunic was of deerskin with an ermine hood. This had cost 39s. – the equivalent of two years' wages for a stone mason or carpenter. Ermine was also used to trim his top cloak, and though we have to imagine a pair of high boots for riding, we know he wore a pair of leather slippers costing 2s. when in the manor. As for his new horse, that was protected against the weather by a coarse russet covering.

Richard ended his first day's journey just down the road at Ledbury. Here the household rested to allow more preparation for the journeys ahead. The farriers attended to the horses and the hounds were sent on to Prestbury, where the adjoining deer park was one of the attractions of the manor. There was a slice of ill luck when William, the head cook, was taken ill just when his skills were needed most, and he was left behind. The burden fell on Adam, his deputy, Little William and their helpers, but they rose to the occasion.

The winter of 1289–90 was mild but particularly wet, and the already slow progress of the party was hampered by mud and puddles in the tracks that served as roads in medieval times. On December 20 the travellers reached Newent for the night, and the next day saw them at Highnam; from there they passed over the Severn by the Westgate causeway at Gloucester, to reach the moated manor house at the bishop's market town of Prestbury on the evening of the 22nd.

At Prestbury all had been prepared under the experienced and watchful eye of one of Richard's most trusted and long-serving bailiffs, Girard de Eugina, who had been conducting the affairs of this manor for the last forty years. His preparations for the great festival were as meticulous as the record of his expenditure kept by the chaplain.

We have already noted the burning of the charcoal and the brewing of the beer overseen by Robert de Calewe. In addition there had been more substantial preparations in the form of building improvements, with chimneys added to the kitchen and the repair of the oven and furnace. The kitchen stood some distance away from the great hall as a precaution against fire, so a covered passage linking the two had been built to prevent the food from cooling too rapidly. At the end of this passage there was a new dresser on which final touches to the food could be made before it was taken in to the guests.

Girard had also bought vast quantities of crockery: three hundred dishes, a hundred and fifty large plates and two hundred small ones, plus a dozen cups. The accounts let us down if we want to know the number of guests who shared the feast, but the number of horses in the stable rose from 41 to 55 on Christmas Eve. It is unlikely that many guests walked.

To modern readers the Christmas menu is staggering in its quantity. Christmas Eve was a time of abstinence before the excesses of the following day, but even so Bishop Richard and his following fed off herrings, codlings, conger eels and eels, plus a salmon of exceptional quality which had cost 5s. 8d., a huge sum. On Christmas Day the feasting began with the entry of the roasted boar, garnished with lemons brought from Ledbury. Then followed two and three-quarter carcases of beef, two calves, four does, four pigs, about sixty fowl, eight partridges, two geese and lashings of bread and cheese, accompanied by ten sextaries – a sextary being seven pints – of red wine, one of white, and unrecorded quantities of beer.

Saffron, mustard, butter and nine hundred eggs complemented the main dishes, but nutritionists will note the absence of vegetables or fruit other than lemons. Perhaps they had been home-produced, and therefore did not appear in the accounts. More probably they simply did not figure, since they were poor man's food, supplemented occasionally by leftovers from the rich man's table.

The consumption of such vast quantities and the recovery from them must have precluded much other activity over Christmas, but we know that Bishop Richard attended mass, for an offertory of 4s. 1d. for the poor is recorded. Other activity is not so sacred, for there are hints that there was hunting in the deer park with the hounds sent from Ledbury. Fourteen does were 'received from the place where they had been put to fatten', which must be a euphemism for hunted in the park! The festivities continued into the 26th and 27th, the feasts of St. Stephen and St. John the Apostle, but then the bishop's journey to London beckoned again.

The route he took is unfamiliar to modern travellers. The party made stops at Coln St. Aldwyns, Faringdon, Wantage, Reading and Bedfont before finally arriving at the bishop's residence at Queenhithe on January 7. Richard de Swinfield's aversion to large public meetings meant that he spent less than a week there before retiring to the country – at Kensington! – for three days. From here he journeyed back to Prestbury, arriving for a month's stay on January 25.

In contrast to the indulgences of Christmas, the household now subjected itself to the comparative self-denial of Lent, the onset of which, on February 15, is recorded in the accounts by the sudden appearance of quantities of milk, cheese, almonds, figs and raisins, in addition to enormous numbers of herrings – 5,900 brought from Gloucester by cart and packhorse over a period of three weeks.

The despatching of the hounds to Ledbury only towards the end of the stay reminds us that hunting in Prestbury Park had continued, though meat was not consumed. Interestingly, the accounts also reveal that during this second stay a rabbit warren was created in the park; the rabbit, farmed for its meat and fur, had not yet become the ubiquitous pest of the modern farmer.

Bishop Richard and his household returned to Ledbury on February 23, and we never again have such a detailed account of any stay in Prestbury. Richard died in 1317, but later bishops continued to visit the manor, and other records allow us to fill in the subsequent history of the site. By 1344 the buildings were in such poor repair that the chapel was completely ruined, and three barns burned down. Repairs were made to enable bishops to pay the occasional visit, but in 1560 the manor passed to Elizabeth I.

In 1643, during the Civil War, it was briefly occupied by the Roundheads, but by 1698 the buildings were dismantled, with some masonry going to repair Prestbury Church. This left two platforms surrounded by neglected moats lying next to the decaying deer park, used first for farming and much later for the famous Cheltenham racecourse.

There the story would have ended if part of the site had not been used by the developers of suburban villas for prosperous Cheltenham businessmen in the early years of this century. The threat to it was such that in 1937 archaeological excavations were started on the platform that had contained the manor house, and five years after a further excavation in 1951 a report was published by Helen O'Neil, a distinguished Gloucestershire county archaeologist. She was able to identify the great hall of Bishop Richard's feast as a two-bay structure, possibly with an upper floor housing the bishop's solar or retiring room at the southern end.

The fascinating part of her report centres on the discovery of the foundations of the passageway built to link the kitchen with the great hall for Christmas, 1289 – and even a structure that could be identified as the remains of the dresser. Also found were the chapel that stood in such decay in 1344, and its successor, as were the Roundheads' lead bullets and clay pipes.

One point that puzzled the excavators was answered by John de Kempsey's account roll. There was an absence of any quantity of pottery from the thirteenth and fourteenth centuries – but in an entry for January 28, 1290, we find the cook purchasing 24 cups for 15d., and 50 dishes, a hundred plates and 50 saucers for 3s. to replace breakages when one of the carts overturned at Lechlade. The bishop obviously took his crockery with him!

The moated site can still be visited at Shaw Green in Prestbury, lying by the perimeter of the racecourse. Now a scheduled monument, it will not suffer again the scare of 1926, when great housing developments were proposed; nevertheless, the casual visitor there today will find it hard to imagine the lively scenes recorded and hinted at by the conscientious de Kempsey seven hundred years ago.

De Spenser's Feast

ADIN WILLIAMS

Some people see Adin Williams, an East Cotswold village schoolmaster of late Victorian times, as a counterpart of his Dundee contemporary William McGonagall. I have to disagree, for while McGonagall's poetry was triumphantly awful, poor old Williams's, all too often, was just plain awful.

I had thought to spare readers all of 'De Spenser's Feast', subtitled 'A Legend of Fairford', and restrict myself to excerpts. But once you have steeled yourself to it it is by no means difficult to read, so I reproduce it here in its entirety.

When the poem first appeared in Williams's Lays and Legends of Gloucestershire — *a subscription volume supported by large numbers of the county set of the day — the poet offered the following foreword:*

'About A.D. 1000, the manor of Fairford belonged to Brihtric, surnamed "the Snow", son of Algar, "Lord of the Honour of Gloucestershire". This Saxon Thane had been sent by the king Edward Confessor, in an embassy to Baldwin of Flanders. Baldwin's daughter Matilda fell in love with Brihtric, and for him refused the hand of William of Normandy. Brihtric refused her love with scorn; then she, hating the Saxon as much as she had before loved him, married William; instigated the conquest of England; took Brihtric prisoner; and starved him to death in prison . . . De Spenser, favourite of Edward II, held the manor of Fairford in 1322.'

129

The heaped-up logs and torches burning bright
Made glad De Spenser's hall that winter night,
Where men at arms and vassals all day long
Had passed the wassail bowl with mirth and song.
At Cirencester Edward held his court,
And kept the season meet with Christmas sport;
His nobles gathered in from town and town
But some went there to meet a kingly frown.
Not so De Spenser; at that gathering,
He 'bove the rest was favoured by the king,
And hated by his peers; for haughty pride,
And evil counsel running side by side
Made England's barons feel the despot's will
More hardly since it wrought to do them ill.
De Spenser purposed, at his Fairford hall,
On New Year's eve his tenants round to call,
That he and they might make a merry feast,
And hail the New Year rising in the east.
For this he left the court, and rode away
Across the fields that 'twixt the places lay,
To Fairford hall, where flocking tenants wait
The coming of the lord in feudal state.
The short, dull day had hastened into night
Before De Spenser's pennons came in sight;
But soon the trumpets, ringing thro' the dark,
Proclaim the cortege passing up the park.
The portal opens, when the warder sees
The mail-clad horsemen 'mong the dusky trees.
The horses champ, the clatt'ring armour rings,
As each one from his saddle gladly springs.
The nobles stride along the rush-strewn hall
And reach the dais, where soft carpets fall
O'er chair and floor, while echoing plaudits greet

Each noble as he takes his rightful seat.
Upon the board the fare they haste to place;
'Tis rich and rare, as ever feast did grace.
The wine is plentiful and strong and red,
The guests have each and all a seasoned head,
And nothing lacked to make the feasters gay,
When all had eaten and the jests made way.

A minstrel old was in the hall that night;
De Spenser met him in a woeful plight
Outside the town, where he had passed that day.
The Baron brought him with them on the way,
And now with food and wine refreshed and strong
The old man stands to cheer them with his song.
His dark eyes glitter in the torches' light,
Upon his shoulders fall his ringlets white,
His cheek is ruddy with a rising flush,
He looks around in the expectant hush.
He holds his harp, well tuned and newly-strung,
He strongly sweeps the trembling chords among
Until a wild and wizard air he wakes,
Which from the strings in fitful murmur breaks.
Then easy preludes sweetly tune his tongue
And linger o'er this ancient song he sung:

   'See the ships are sailing away
   Over the billows white!
   All are sweeping into the bay,
   Bound for Flanders' court today,
   Baldwin, famed for wealth and might,
   Looks for them to come e'er night;
   Ambassadors are they.

   'Brihtric, Algar's son did go,

131

Peer of all,
Brihtric, named by some "the Snow",
He was so white and tall.
He had left his heart behind,
He to maiden's charms was blind,
Dazzled by fair Edith's face –
Edith, famed for swanly grace,
With her heart on Harold set;
Brihtric ne'er a thought did get,
But he loved her none the less,
Vainly sighed in vain regret
In a lovesick loneliness.

'Thro' the massive palace gate
Go they now.
On the lordly Baldwin wait,
And the noble lords to the ladies bow,
All in state.
And Brihtric, the youngest and fairest there,
With a brow so clear,
Gazed on the bevy of lovely dames
With a careless eye that no beauty shames.
But Baldwin's daughter, with eyes like fire
Looked into his with warm desire.
Matilda, wooed by the kings around,
Loved where no love for her was found.
While her suitors came and wooed in vain
She set her thought on the Saxon Thane.
She tried to win him from day to day,
But he coldly turned and mocked her sway.
Then she awoke to a woman's scorn,
And out of her love a hate was born.
She had shown herself as a woman won,
And the winner despised the easy prize.

She vowed deep vengeance for what he had done,
For a woman's hatred never dies.

'Harold is dead and defeated,
The Saxons have made their last stand.
The conquest is sure and completed,
And William is lord of the land.
From the battlefield Brihtric had taken
Edith, the swan-necked, after the fray,
Her Harold she had not forsaken,
Cloistered she lived to mourn for that day.

'And Matilda, who had loved so late,
Was William's wife, with regal state,
Nor was she slow to understand
That all the pow'r was in her hand.
For now her hate on Brihtric's head
Could pour its venom sharp and dread,
And he had fought and battled well
Around the flag where Harold fell,
And scorning flight that turned to yield
Was beaten, driven from the field.
Then 'mong a few remaining Thanes,
He lurked within the woods and plains.
But soon the vengeful Queen sent round
Keen searchers that his hiding found.
Her soldiers tracked him fled to Kent,
And soon in prison he is pent,
Where slowly wasting day by day,
They starved his bitter life away.
The heart that owned him once its joy
Was panting, eager to destroy.

'The slighted woman found above his grave

133

The satisfaction she had sought for years.
And he so fair, so noble and so brave
Left mem'ries shrined in England's bitter tears.'

He ended, and the clamour, long suppressed,
Broke from the throat of each applauding guest.
The torches flickered, and the firelight dim
Bespoke the Old year on the New year's rim.
The drinkers, dozing, felt the silence fall,
And slumb'ring forms soon filled the dark'ning hall.

*It was in 1321 that Edward II spent Christmas at
Cirencester, during the depths of his war against the
barons, who were particularly strong in the Welsh borders
and Gloucester. The favour he showed such unworthy
recipients as Piers Gaveston and the De Spensers was a key
point of contention, but his star was still rising as he made
his way to Cirencester; he had recently taken Leeds Castle
and won several more barons over on his march westwards,
gathering fresh troops as he did so.*

*He met his brothers Thomas, the Earl Marshal and
Edmund, Earl of Kent, at Cirencester, several more barons
submitted to him there, including the Mortimers, and by
the end of the campaign the De Spensers were restored to all
their former privileges. Their fortune was not to hold, and
when the Queen's revolt began to bite they were among the
first to be executed. As for Edward II, as we record
elsewhere in this book, his next Christmas journey through
Gloucestershire, six years on, was tragically different from
this one.*

from

Jump For Joy

PAT SMYTHE

Pat Smythe of Miserden was a sporting superstar of the early 1950s, a horsewoman who attracted far more attention and adulation than Lucinda Prior-Palmer and Virginia Holgate in more recent years. This short section from her autobiography captures some of the excitement of those times; it is Christmas, 1953, and she is looking back on the highspots of an extended show jumping tour of the United States and Canada.

It all began when the show jumping ended. With Shirley Thomas, I toured the eastern states from Canada south to Savannah in Georgia, on to Miami and along the Florida coast. With Shirley, too, I air-taxied back to Ottawa for Christmas. I won the horn-blowing competition, with an atrocious performance, at Ottawa's Hunt Ball.

On New Year's Eve I dined in Rockford, Illinois, fifty miles west of Chicago – with a plateful of roast beef and Yorkshire pudding. I drank my champagne toast to 1954 beside the northern waters of the Mississippi, a thousand miles from where the old river of jazz band steamboats flows past New Orleans.

I shot a horned hoot-owl out west in Texas, hunted the fox

back east in Virginia, and searched for trinkets in Syracuse. With Ralph, my cousin, I flew across rich corn lands and empty deserts, in the sun, in the darkness, in fog, rain and icy wind. I sweated on the dusty prairie and shivered in the mountains. I rode a yellow mustang through ten hours of a Texas day. I drank thick, scalding coffee from a saucer on the ranch, and sipped cool Martinis in the city. I met four millionaires with gold rings on their fingers, trouble on their minds; Mexican peasants with holes in their shirts, sun in their veins; and hard-riding cowboys with cattle to tame and songs to sing.

Back in England friends would ask: 'Did you enjoy the trip?' To which I would reply: 'Yes, it was lovely, thanks . . .' And as those weeks of high experience flashed through the mind's eye I thought how odd, to sum it all up with the polite formalities of suburban good manners.

Mum's the Word

MICHAEL HARDCASTLE

Best known as a prolific author of books for children and young people, Michael Hardcastle has also written extensively about the people and places of the West Country. This portrait of the Marshfield Mummers was first published in 1977.

On Boxing Day morning motorists will once again stream into Marshfield in great numbers. They will be arriving, some from as far afield as London – '103 miles to Hyde Park Corner', as a plaque in the High Street points out – to witness the annual performance of the famed Marshfield Mummers; and some drivers will doubtless remember the days, only a decade ago, when the main street was congested for a different reason. As many inhabitants recall with a shudder, until the bypass was opened Marshfield was a notorious bottleneck on the highway from Bristol to Chippenham.

The Mummers are seven local men, including a couple of garage proprietors and a farmer, attired in costumes of tattered newsprint and coloured paper that sometimes earn them the tag of the 'paper boys'. What they are performing is an ancient fertility rite. Based on a legend of George and the Dragon, but with the central character now King William, it is unique, for it was never recorded in print by any antiquarian when originally staged in Marshfield. During the later part of the last century the play lapsed, and would have passed into obscurity but for a remarkable coincidence at the beginning of the 1930s.

The then Vicar of Marshfield one day overheard his gardener quoting certain mysterious lines; intrigued, he called in his sister, a noted folklorist, and she identified them as lines from a St. George play. She gathered around her several villagers, and between them they pieced together the old Marshfield version, which was then revived for public showing the following Christmas. Lasting about seven minutes, and performed four times in the hour from 11 a.m. at strategic points from the Market Square to the Almshouses, it nowadays commands a great following and pulls in visitors in increasing numbers – to say nothing of the money it raises for charity.

'People *fight* to put money in the collecting boxes,' reports

The Marshfield Mummers fall in behind their bellman.

Some bizarre characters catch the eye in this mumming group
from Thornbury early this century.

Raymond Rawlings with a degree of astonishment. A retired
postman it is he, dressed in a long black overcoat and top hat,
and carrying a handbell, who leads the Mummers to their
several stages and formally introduces the show. 'Your hands

'Who bist thee as can't be hit, With thy gurt yud and little wit?' Dr Do-No-Good stands between Belzebub and Johnny Dout in this Fairford mumming play of the early 1980s.

can get terribly cold, and once I thought I'd borrow some gloves. But at the rehearsal the bell fell out of my hand and slithered right across the church hall. Just imagine! Someone said I'd dropped a clanger. I never wore gloves again.'

Dr. Zeta Eastes has long been the Mummers' 'mascot and publicist – or better still, their Fairy Godmother, as I like to think of it.' She says that they sometimes remark that they continue to perform the play only because so many people come to see it, 'but I don't think that's true. They have a feeling that it has got to be done. It's part of their inheritance. They used to do it when hardly anyone was watching, so the crowds are not the relevant factor.'

The meetings of the Mummers, when it is decided how the

money they have raised should be divided among charities, are held not in the bar that bears their name at the Crown Inn but in 'Mrs. Doctor's' house. One Christmas, because of snow, the play was staged on her lawn, and it became a tradition for her to reward the Mummers with glasses of hot rum and ginger. Spectators were delighted to have a free drink, too, but eventually it became too much of a good thing. 'When it got to the point when complete strangers were putting their glasses back on the tray over my shoulder and saying "Thanks, I'll have another of those", I decided that was it, finish.'

Among other groups active in the Cotswolds are the City of Gloucester Mummers, whose Boxing Day morning performances with the Gloucestershire Morrismen have become a big

The Gloucestershire Morris Men are traditional visitors to Gloucester and Cheltenham on Boxing Day.

draw in Gloucester and Cheltenham over the past two decades; the Waterley Bottom Mummers, noted more fully in this book in the section by Carol Wright, who concentrate chiefly on pub performances in the Dursley area in the nights leading up to Christmas; and the Kempsford Mummers, welcome visitors to several East Gloucestershire pubs as the holiday season approaches.

The latter group was reformed in 1983 by a couple living in the former home of Cecil King, who ran a previous mumming troupe in Kempsford up until the early 1950s. Their text dates from 1931, with modifications, and it is unusual in including Robin Hood and a costumed dragon among its characters.

Pantomime Favourites

Gloucestershire can lay firm claim to one of the characters who will be delighting audiences up and down the country during this winter's pantomime season – and take credit for introducing another to the world.

Dick Whittington ranks as one of the county's most famous sons. Born at Pauntley Court in the mid-fourteenth century, this was no poor boy; he was the third son of Sir William

Pauntley Court, the much-changed home of Dick
Whittington.

Whittington, one of a long line of prosperous West Country
landowners, and his mother Lady Joan was the widow of
Thomas de Berkeley of Coberley, a relative of the powerful
lords of Berkeley Castle. There is evidence to suggest,
however, that Sir William fell out of favour with the Crown,
and as he died when Dick was only 14 it could well have been
that this third son from the remote West did not present too
prepossessing an image when he reached London.

Perhaps unsurprisingly at a time when Gloucestershire was
internationally important in the woollen industry, Dick
entered the textile trade and made his mark as a mercer, or
dealer in silks and velvets. Then, as now, the politics of the
City of London were closely enmeshed in the ancient trade
guilds, and Dick did indeed rise through the ranks to gain a
knighthood and become mayor – the title Lord Mayor was not
then in use – in 1397, 1406 and 1419.

The legend of the poor boy and the cat first emerged in print
in 1605, in a play *The History Of Richard Whittington*. There is
no historical evidence for the bells calling him to turn again or
indeed for the cat, though there are ingenious theories that
suggest that this could be a nickname for the barges that
carried Dick's wares up and down the Thames, or for a
campaign he introduced to drive rats out of the city.

The latter is possible for Richard Whittington was a forceful reformer, leaving money to rebuild Newgate Prison and the remainder of his fortune to other charitable causes. In one point myth and reality meet in that Dick did indeed fall in love with and marry Alice Fitzwaryn, daughter of a rich Dorset knight. But unhappily for panto fans, I have unearthed no proof that she was a dab hand at singing *On A Wonderful Day Like Today*.

Gloucestershire's other key figure in pantomime history, in a rather more obscure manner than Dick Whittington, is Thomas Dover, who spent his later years at Stanway House. His claim to fame is that he rescued the shipwrecked sailor whose story inspired Daniel Defoe to write Robinson Crusoe.

Thomas was a grandson of Robert Dover, founder of the Cotswold Games on the uplands still known as Dover's Hill above Chipping Campden. But if anything he led an even more colourful life than his ancestor, with his seafaring exploits only a fragment of the picture.

After gaining a B.A. at Oxford in 1684 Thomas Dover went on to study 'physic' and set up in medical practice in Bristol, where he soon made a speciality – and a small fortune – out of treating syphilis with metallic mercury. This cure had an unfortunate side-effect which saw several patients die of mercurial poisoning, but Dover rejoiced in his nickname of Doctor Quicksilver, and by his mid-forties he was looking for further means of making his money work for him.

Like many a respectable Bristol businessman before and since he turned to privateering, a legal form of piracy in which individuals applied to the Crown for 'Letters of Marque and Reprisal' that allowed them to attack enemy craft on the high seas in return for a share of the booty.

He fitted out two frigates, the *Duke* and *Duchess*, and while he went for experience in recruiting the notorious privateer Woodes Rogers to lead his expedition, he raised many

eyebrows in Bristol by taking personal command of the second ship, the *Duke*.

The party set sail in August 1708, and it was three years before Dover returned with a personal profit of £170,000. The War of the Spanish Succession was still raging, so his ships were free to attack French men-of-war as well as the traditional cannon-fodder, Spanish merchantmen off central America.

Today, however, we remember that voyage only for its Crusoe connections. As night descended on January 21, 1709 the ships were off the apparently uninhabited Pacific island of Juan Fernandez. Several crew members were stricken with scurvy, meat and fruit supplies were low and Dover was being rowed ashore in the gathering gloom when a light flickered on the island. His men insisted on postponing the landing until morning – and it was then that they encountered Alexander Selkirk of Largs, a sailor who had been marooned there for four years and four months.

In Bristol tradition has it that Defoe first heard this classic travellers' tale in the Llandoger Trow, the half-timbered pub down by Welsh Back that gives us some idea of the seaport of old. Doubtless every sea-dog in the city, for years after the event, claimed to have been on the shore of Juan Fernandez that morning, just as you cannot to this day walk into a bar in Swansea without bumping into a man who is owed half-a-crown by Dylan Thomas.

That, then, is Thomas Dover's most romantic claim to fame, but it is not the only reason his name has lived on for so long after his death in Stanway in 1742. Returning to medicine after his adventures, he distinguished himself by formulating Dover's Powder, a remedy for diarrhoea that is available on prescription to this day. The fact would doubtless delight many of the music hall and variety comedians who have made their mark on the pantomime stage over the years.

Christmas Day in the Workhouse

DAVID ALDRED

It is Christmas Day in the Workhouse,
And the cold bare walls are bright
With garlands of green and holly,
And the place is a pleasant sight:
For with clean-washed hands and faces,
In a long and hungry line
The paupers sit at the tables,
For this is the hour they dine . . .

. . . And so on for another couple of dozen verses, but in spite of its tum-ti-tum rhythm and its openness to parody, there is nothing remotely funny about George R. Sims's savage indictment of a Poor Law that survived for nearly a hundred years, from 1834 to 1929.

The 1834 Act grouped parishes together into unions, with boards of guardians elected by ratepayers to levy and spend the poor rate. Union workhouses were built to house the paupers in those days before the Welfare State – and it was the express intention of the Act to ensure that conditions in the institutions would be worse than those of the poorest labourer.

This meant a loss of personal freedom, segregation by age and sex, drab clothes, a drab diet, and a harsh discipline revolving around such work as stone- and bone-crushing, oakum-picking – unravelling old rope – cleaning the work-house and washing clothes. The only times of relief were Sundays, Good Friday and, most of all, Christmas Day. Between 1834 and 1929 there were more than ninety Christ-mases in the sixteen workhouses of the old county of Glou-cestershire. Records give us an inkling of what some of them were like.

In 1849 the Winchcombe guardians were approached by the workhouse inmates to provide some extras for Christmas Day. In granting the request they stipulated that not more than a sovereign should be spent, a sum which would not have gone far even in those days. Poor Law records are full of such examples of board members regarding themselves as guardians of the rates, rather than of the poor.

The guardians at Northleach, however, seem to have been more generous. In 1877, the year that Sims's ballad appeared, the inmates dined off beef, beer and plum pudding. At Dursley the previous year the guardians had allowed the workhouse master to spend £4 5s. 0d. on providing 'a better diet than usual on Christmas Day, and a goose for the officers'. This did not include the drink, for he later presented, and had passed, a bill for £8 2s. 0d. for beer and 14s. 9d. for wine. No doubt the people in his charge were able to forget, for a few hours at least, the stigma of a workhouse existence. Even in 1855 the master had been allowed £4 to spend on Christmas Day; inflation was less of a problem then.

There are many references in the guardians' records to allowing 'the usual extras' for Christmas dinner, without being more specific, but in 1904 the Cheltenham board gave firm instructions that the Christmas beer allowance was to be 'Half a pint at Lunch time (10 a.m.) on Boxing Day and Half a pint with Christmas Dinner'. At Thornbury in 1908 the visitors commented that 'The Christmas fare looked good and appe-tising . . . We wish them all a merry Christmas season'. The visit, in fact, was made on Christmas Eve; Christmas Day in the workhouse was not always December 25!

There was, however, a regular visitor on that date – the union chaplain; the inmates were never allowed to forget the religious significance of Christmas. The Gloucestershire chaplains, on the whole, seem to have conducted their duties conscientiously. Of course they had a captive audience, but not one noted for the strength of its religious conviction.

In fact early in 1848 the Winchcombe guardians, having struggled through Christmas after the resignation of the vicar as their chaplain, decided to do away with the position altogether because there was so little demand from the inmates. The problem was resolved only later in the year, when the bishop allowed the vicar to use the union's £40 salary to pay a curate.

In 1851 the Rev. C. H. Davis started a long career as chaplain to the Stroud Union. On Christmas Day he took morning service and gave communion to six male and seven female paupers, and his first years were a struggle. In his report the following Christmas he wrote that he was forced to note 'the *total idleness* and *mental inactivity*' of the old, who would be better off 'making clothes pegs, netting etc. to occupy time. Idleness being the parent of evil'. By 1854, happily, he was able to report a dramatic improvement.

As the nineteenth century progressed the harshness of the workhouse regime was softened. From 1889 the boarding-out of pauper children was encouraged, from 1892 tobacco and snuff were officially allowed to elderly men, and from 1894 their female counterparts were given an extra tea allowance. The workhouse also began to attract private charity, especially at Christmas, and the inmates at Winchcombe were particularly fortunate.

Here local benefactors, headed inevitably by the philanthropic Mrs. Emma Dent of Sudeley Castle, competed with each other in their benevolence. In 1895 she provided tea, sugar, sweets, oranges, nuts, tobacco and cake, while Mrs. Adlard of Postlip Hall sent tea, tobacco and cakes. Further gifts of raisins, almonds, toys, pictures and cards were provided by other local worthies.

The following Christmas at Winchcombe the chaplain and his wife laid on a tea and concert, and not to be outdone, the Wesley Guild of the local chapel offered similar hospitality for Christmas, 1897. The guardians required full details of this doubtful Nonconformist enterprise, however, and this delayed the event until January 21!

In 1903 the *Cheltenham Chronicle and Graphic* brought Christmas Day in the town's workhouse into its readers' homes, with a picture feature on the various wards. Looking at the photographs today the fresh flowers on the tables and seasonal wall decorations contrast sadly with the standard-issue dark capes, light skirts and white linen caps of the haggard old women inmates, drained of their self-respect.

The last Christmas Day in the workhouse was in 1928, and

A Gloucestershire Royal Infirmary ward, *c*. 1900.

Christmas cheer for the workers at Marling and Evans's mill at
Stroud, 1935.

early in 1929 the clerk to the Gloucester Union submitted his
final report. Twenty-five Christmas parcels had been distributed to inmates 'through the kindness of Lonsdale Women's
Meeting'. I hope George R. Sims would have approved of that.

The Duke of Buckingham's Christmas, 1507

N. F. LARGE

Bounteous Buckingham, Shakespeare called him, and Edward Stafford, the third duke, certainly knew how to entertain on the grand scale. The survival of a fragment of his household accounts has ensured that his Christmas festivities at Thornbury Castle in 1507 are now firmly entrenched in local folklore, not least because they reveal a side of his nature that ultimately led to his undoing.

His guest list is impressive:

Thornbury the feast of the Nativity.
Saturday, December 25.

> Dined . . . 95 Gentry.
> 107 Yeomen.
> 97 Garcons.
>
> Supped . . . 84 Gentry.
> 114 Yeomen.
> 92 Garcons.

And what dining and supping. There was Gascony wine,

'Bounteous' Buckingham.

Rhenish and Malvoisey, ale and beer in bewildering quantities, and a meat list that was not only massive, but which included such delicacies as a peacock bought for 2s. and game ranging from mallard and widgeon to snipe and woodcock. Most of the serious eating, however, was catered for by one carcase and 20 rounds of beef (20s.), nine carcases of mutton (16s.), four pigs (8s.), 1½ calves (4s.), plus swans, geese, suckling pigs, capons, chickens, rabbits and twelve dubious sounding 'large birds'. Four hundred eggs, 491 loaves and twenty dishes of butter helped ensure that no-one went hungry in between times.

The motives for a spread of this size were several. Bounteous the duke – then in his prime, in his 30th year – may have been, but it was not pure magnanimity. He was a considerable landowner, with property in other parts of the country, and among the guests were four bailiffs who had brought him rent. The duke was to become Chief Constable of England and an apparent friend of Henry VIII who was popular among his fellow nobles. No doubt some of them stayed on for hunting after Christmas, or perhaps for jousting in the tilt field between Gloucester Road and Castle Street. We know that among those who sat down to dine were two minstrels, six trumpeters and a 27-voice male choir, and the appearance of a bear as the recipient of two loaves suggests that baiting was part of the entertainment.

Buckingham was an ambitious man, and could have had designs on the throne. If this was so, entertaining on a grand scale might have been one means of gaining support for an ultimate revolt against the king. Henry was not unaware of the danger, though, and with his suspicions fanned perhaps by Cardinal Wolsey, he summoned the duke to London and imprisoned him on a charge of treason.

From his portrait, the third Duke of Buckingham has the air of a man who enjoyed his food. Christmas, 1507, must have been a pleasurable time for him. Perhaps he even recalled it on that fateful morning, fourteen years later, when he kept his appointment with the headsman on Tower Hill.

Bump in the Night

A spooky tale's best for winter, whatever Shakespeare had to say on the subject, and the Cotswolds abound in them. Two villages in particular can claim more than a skeleton staff of spectral monks, musicians and headless horsemen, but stage-coaches are often on people's minds at Christmas, so we shall begin our spine-tingling travels with them.

The Puesdown Inn, on the A40 near Northleach, is the scene of much activity. Very close to it a track leaves the main road eastwards, and it once served as an alternative route for coaches along this main road to London when the marshy valley road became impassable. A woman driver from Charlton Kings and her passenger have reported two sightings of a coach and four emerging from this track, crossing the A40 and continuing into woodland opposite. She could even tell the colour of the horses.

At the Puesdown Inn itself, a lonely spot also associated with highwaymen and strandings in winter snow, a ghost, possibly that of a wounded poacher, has been known to knock on the door late and long. A former landlady found the ordeal particularly harrowing.

But back on the road, and a tale from an avid local ghost hunter of recent years, the late Wilfred Cox of Cheltenham:

'In 1972 Mr. W. Jefferies of Cheltenham was driving a delivery van home along the A417, Ermine Street, in early dusk at 5.30 p.m. He had passed the Highwayman, formerly the Mason's Arms, and had reached the approaches to the Syde turning when, to his astonishment, a white coach drawn by four white horses crossed the road obliquely some 15 yards ahead of him. It was so close that it forced him to brake hard.

'There are two interesting features of this stretch of road, apart from its Roman and possibly prehistoric origins. A minor road crosses the Syde road and used to meet Ermine Street at an angle at what was called Smith's Crossing before aiming for Elkstone. An old cottage stood at this spot before the road was altered.

'It was close to here that the Gifford family waylaid a treasure train belonging to Edward II, an act that brought the demolition of their castle at Brimpsfield as retribution.'

Other stagecoach traditions flourish around Burford, while a few years ago a couple of lads swore they saw a coach descending one of the narrow lanes down to Woodchester from Minchinhampton Common, near Stroud. And in 1980 a Bishop's Cleeve man saw a coach complete with horses and passengers emerging from a long blocked-up archway in the wall of the Farmer's Arms pub on the Cheltenham–Evesham road close to his home.

Back on the A40 at Hangman's Stone, close to Compton Abdale, a spectral horse and trap has been blamed for many single-vehicle accidents in which drivers have swerved into the verge. One night during the last war Mr. Anderson, the special constable for Compton Abdale, telephoned Northleach police station to report just such a mishap. 'I expect he saw the trap,' was the terse and unsurprised reply. Visits by phantom carriages are also an occupational hazard of living in large country houses with Chavenage, near Tetbury and Nether Lypiatt Manor, near Stroud, being particularly susceptible.

Prestbury's cast-list of ghosts is impressive, with at least half a dozen of them according to Tudor Williams, who has studied the evidence. All seem amiable enough souls apart from a strangler in a seventeenth-century farmhouse at Cleeve Corner. Some visitors staying there have woken with a strange feeling of dread, clamminess and the sensation of a hand so tight around their neck that they cannot even call for help. The theory is that it is the ghost of a burglar who throttled a young bride in her bed, made off with her wedding gifts – but left his troubled soul for ever more.

Another Prestbury personality is a Black Abbot who glides down the High Street from the church to a piece of ground used as a cemetery by the village's medieval priory, and then turns towards the beautiful thatched Reform Cottage, which was once a village barn. A monk has also been seen close to the racecourse on the site of the medieval Bishop of Hereford's moated manor, scene of spectacular Christmas festivities recorded elsewhere in this book.

At Walnut Cottage in Tatchley Lane, Old Moses and his horse were seen several times in 1961, when alterations were being made to this former stable. 'I'm Old Moses,' he is reputed to have said. 'You see, I like to look in sometimes.' He looks like a groom, but he was a former trainer who is believed to have been murdered in the loft.

Sundial Cottage in The Burgage plays host to a girl playing the spinet, though in more recent times only the music has been heard; there is talk of a knight in rusty armour riding a wizened horse who canters along until he stops suddenly, almost falls, then salutes and continues on his way; the road between the churchyard and the Plough Inn strikes some bypassers as particularly melancholy; an old lady in archaic clothes has been seen looking in the High Street shop windows; not many winters ago a Bishop's Cleeve man saw a cyclist in 1930s dress riding down the hill towards the village from Southam; and up on Cleeve Common, the spectre of the headless horseman is known far beyond the Prestbury parish boundaries.

'Perhaps most dramatic of all is the ghost of the cavalier, of which there are two versions,' says Tudor Williams. 'One has it that he was a messenger to the camp of Edward IV at Tewkesbury in 1471, shot by an archer. In spring hoofbeats have been heard and the faint outline of a horse and rider seen, before both are suddenly cut off. A tall tale? Perhaps, but in 1901, when roadmen were working in Shaw Green Lane, a skeleton was unearthed with an arrow in its chest. . . .

'For the second version of the cavalier we go back to The Burgage, where there have also been reports of hoofbeats which stop suddenly. This is said to be the ghost of a Royalist despatch rider racing between Sudeley Castle and Gloucester, a route for which the Burgage would have been a main thoroughfare. The tale is that a trap had been set by a rope stretched across the road, and as the luckless horseman fell he was set upon by the rebels.

'What I do know is that I was walking my dog along The Burgage one night when he suddenly shot back across the road to me in tremendous haste. I told a friend, and he said: "Maybe he saw a ghost." Maybe he did, but in Prestbury you've got to ask yourself – which one?'

In Kempsford, where the Thames flows towards the Wiltshire plains, the confusion of ghostly visitors is compounded by the fact that there appear to be two spectral ladies called Maud. One was betrothed to Edward I, who held court at Kempsford Castle, but after his death she married Henry, Duke of Lancaster, Baron of Kempsford from 1336. After their son and heir drowned in the ford Henry was so distraught that he fled the village – a shoe cast by his horse in flight is to be seen nailed to the church door to this day – and Maud is still to be heard by the river bank, bewailing her double loss.

A pale, wraith-like figure is also to be seen not far away, along Lady Maud's Walk, a riverside terrace in the grounds of the Old Vicarage, which stands on the site of Kempsford

Castle. June R. Lewis, one of the finest contemporary chroniclers of the Cotswolds, swears that during the last war members of the Home Guard would patrol the walk only in pairs, and she takes up the story:

'Like many a family divided by civil strife, Lady Maud's husband and brother were on opposing sides during the barons' uprising against Edward II. One storm-swept night Lady Maud's brother arrived at the castle seeking refuge; her husband was away fighting and she hid him in a secret room at the foot of the battlements, smuggling food to him under cover of darkness. A knight whose advances she had spurned heard a man's voice coming from the cell, and when her husband returned he told him that she was having a clandestine affair.

'Enraged, he traced Maud to the room, struck down her brother and threw her over the battlements into the Thames.

The Puesdown Inn is famous for snow as well as spooks.

When the truth emerged he became a penitent monk – and apart from Lady Maud lamenting her undeserved fate along her walk, both the knight and the monk haunt the Old Vicarage.'

Another resident of that somewhat overcrowded house is the Blue Boy, a phantom child who sits in a velvet 'Bubbles' suit in an equally spectral winged chair in the drawing room. There is speculation that he is the ghost of a youthful Lord Coleraine, a Regency rake with a passion for blue, who was buried above ground to prevent the devil from snatching him.

More humble is the shade of a nursemaid in eighteenth-century dress who carries a baby down the servants' staircase; and when June Lewis visited the Old Vicarage in 1985, the nine-year-old boy of the young family living there told her in completely matter-of-fact tones of the tall man with a high black hat and long coat he had seen in the back corridor, and later walking through the wall of his sister's room. 'It's a wonder they don't all collide,' says Miss Lewis, who nevertheless found the Old Vicarage a warm and welcoming family home.

Cold, Cold Snow

STEVEN BLAKE

The Cotswolds' worst winter in living memory? For big snows it is probably a toss-up between two momentous March falls, in 1916 and 1947. For sheer grinding misery, however, month after month, nothing can touch the big freeze we thought would never go away in 1963.

As we are wont to remark when we see Christmas card scenes of ox-roasts on the Thames, they don't tend to make winters like that today. But they certainly did in 1674, when a snowbound family near Bath survived on grain for three days and nights, and a newly married baker and his bride from Tewkesbury perished while riding out to see friends, 'chilled with cold eternal sleep in sheets of snow wherein they were afterwards found dead, embracing each other.'

The West Country was also devastated in 1683, when 'a mighty great frost the like was not seen in England for many years' lasted from Christmas to Lady Day, and snow lay on some north-facing uplands until well into the summer. Old and infirm people died at an alarming rate, and with the ground 'like rock' as deep as two feet it was an unhappy winter for churchyard sextons.

Christmas 1739 was another unhappy time, preceding the worst winter of that century and the most severe since 1698.

Small boy, big snows, Bisley, March 1916.

159

The *Gloucester Journal* reported that the roads were 'so deep in snow at present that the course of the posts is interrupted', while a poor man of the city, 'supposed to be in liquor', was frozen to death in a brewhouse. He was one of many 'too numerous to mention here who have perished through the extreme severity of the season'.

By a cruel irony, 'the Severn being froze up, a stop is put to the passage of vessels from Shropshire and Worcestershire,' which forced up the price of coal when it was needed most. Salt from Droitwich, too, was in short supply, and prices soared. The extreme cold, which even killed a post boy when he was riding on the North Road, was a 'grievance of the first size', and everywhere there were 'starving poor wretches in droves begging the charity of well-disposed citizens'.

'This winter it begun on the 24th day of December and continued very hard till the end of February, so that very little work could be done,' said the register book for Kingswood, near Wotton-under-Edge, for 1740. And the *Gloucester Journal* for January 15 recorded dire news from Bristol: 'A few days ago a poor woman, who lived in Milk Street, perished with cold after she had been delivered . . . Saturday last a poor man who begged about the streets was found perished to death . . . The vessels and boats at the quay and back are frozen up, as are all the mills up the river, and some of the colliers' horses have dropped down dead with their burdens.'

On February 5 the same newspaper reported a grain vessel frozen in the Severn – and from Thornbury came news that shoals of fish and eels were frozen in the mud along the shore, with local people vying with crows for the pick of the catch. Around Tewkesbury the river was frozen hard enough for horses and wagons to be driven on it, and there were traditional sheep roasts on the ice at Key Bridge and on the quay at Gloucester. It was not until February 20 that the first barge since Christmas sailed down from Worcester, and even when it was thawing and breaking up, ice on the river was a foot thick.

It became fashionable to donate to the needy. Sir Thomas Read gave £60 to relieve the poor of Cricklade, a subscription in Gloucester paid out weekly, and Viscount Gage and others took care of Tewkesbury. One provided 400 sixpenny loaves to be handed out on three successive Sundays, as well as 50 guineas for 'the silent poor'.

But as a postscript to 1740, perhaps the most wretched tale comes not from the early part of the year but the much milder December of the following winter. Then a report from Bristol in the *Journal* tells of a poor woman who 'perished with the cold in the Horse Fair. She was almost naked, and pelted with snowballs a little before she died by a parcel of wicked boys – the unhappy effects of a loose education. . . .'

The road between Bisley and Eastcombe in the notorious winter of 1963.

Judas Fires

The Twelfth Night custom of lighting fires to the twelve apostles – and immediately stamping out the one dedicated to Judas Iscariot – is one that survived into living memory. It was seen as insurance against a poor harvest in the following autumn, and the fact that records tell of the fires being lit 'at the end of twelve lands' suggests that it goes back at least to the days of medieval strip farming.

The usual form was for a large fire representing Christ to be surrounded by twelve small ones. After the Judas fire had been extinguished and its ashes scattered, the others would be watched with interest, and various omens about the coming year would be drawn from the way in which they burned.

A little over a hundred years ago, in *Gloucestershire Notes and Queries* of 1881, the ritual was reported to be 'still customary in some parts of England'.

'This custom was once kept up with much spirit, and oftentimes as many as sixty of these fires might be seen burning at once,' it continued. 'At Pauntley, in Gloucestershire, and the surrounding neighbourhood the servants of each farmer used formerly to assemble in one of the fields that had been sown with grain. Twelve fires with straw were then made in a row, around one of which, much larger than the rest, the servants drank a cheerful glass of cider to their master's health, and success to the future harvest. Afterwards, on their return home, they feasted on cakes soaked in cider, which they claimed as their reward for sowing the grain.'

Much of this information was drawn from Fosbrooke's

Gloucestershire of 1807, while a book published in 1874, Blount's *Tenures of Land and Customs of Manors* described the custom as still prevalent in the neighbouring community of Newent; it was obviously particularly strong in this corner of the county. Blount said the fires were built on the edge of wheat fields in the most elevated spot, while the cakes were 'made of carraway etc. and soaked in cider'.

Twelfth Night generally was celebrated with great enthusiasm until comparatively recently, the Twelfth Cake and its associated customs being the centre of activity. In 1813 Mrs. Mary Yorke, wife of the Bishop of Gloucester, wrote of her Twelfth Cake 'with all the younger folk of the neighbourhood to choose their king and queen according to old custom'; and in 1890 Mrs. Emma Dent of Sudeley Castle recalled 'the good times we had over the Twelfth Cake, and even gingerbread kings and queens covered with glorious apparel in the form of shining gold paper.'

In some families the Twelfth Cake, ceremoniously cut during a lull in the party, contained a dried bean and pea. Traditionally, the man who discovered the bean in his slice of cake was king for the evening, with the girl who found the pea his queen; all of which suggests a certain amount of sorting out of slices before the plates were handed round.

At Sudeley things were done a little differently. 'The "characters" were drawn,' Emma Dent wrote, 'the ladies' out of a good old-fashioned "reticule", the gentlemen's out of a hat. The bliss of drawing No. 1 for king, No. 2 for queen, and so on. Then, after the drawing, came the reading of the verses belonging to each character. I remember on one occasion, when it was my luck to draw the queen, the rapture of having a glittering crown placed on my head, and walking up and down the dancing room with my also glitteringly-crowned young king.'

Occasionally a coin was substituted for the king's bean.

Whoever picked it had to go all over the house making the sign of the cross on all the beams and rafters as a charm against evil before taking on his more jolly monarchal duties.

It could well be that customs such as these, and the Lords of Misrule who once held sway in some households from All Hallows' Eve to Candlemas, stem from the bawdy Saturnalia of Roman times. In this, masters and slaves changed roles – a tradition faintly upheld in the armed forces to this day, when the officers serve the men with Christmas dinner. What is of especial interest in the Twelfth Cake folklore is the way in which the Roman kings of the Saturnalia were elected – by bean lottery. . . .

from

Cider with Rosie

LAURIE LEE

This second excerpt from Laurie Lee's classic takes us to Slad's annual village revels at around the time of Twelfth Night; rich in affectionate humour, it has long been among my favourite passages of that wonderful book.

The Parochial Church Tea and Annual Entertainment was the village's winter treat. It took place in the schoolroom, round

about Twelfth Night, and cost us a shilling to go. The Tea was
an orgy of communal gluttony, in which everyone took pains
to eat more than his money's worth and the helpers ate more
than the customers. The Entertainment which followed, home
produced and by lamplight, provided us with sufficient
catch-phrases for a year.

Regularly, for a few weeks before the night, one witnessed
the same scenes in our kitchen, the sisters sitting in various
corners of the room, muttering secretly to themselves,
smiling, nodding and making lah-di-dah gestures with a kind
of intent and solitary madness. They were rehearsing their
sketches for the Entertainment, which I found impossible not
to learn too, so that I would be haunted for days by three
nightmare monologues full of one-sided unanswered questions.

On the morning of the feast we got the school ready. We
built a stage out of trestles and planks. Mr. Robinson was in
the cloakroom slicing boiled ham, where he'd been for the last
three days, and three giggling helpers were now forking the
meat and slapping it into sandwiches. Outside in the yard
John Barraclough had arrived and set up his old field kitchen,
had broken six hurdles across his knee, and filled up the boiler
with water. Laid out on the wall were thirty-five teapots,
freshly washed and drying in the wind. The feast was
preparing; and by carrying chairs, helping with the stage, and
fetching water from the spring, Jack and I made ourselves
sufficiently noticeable to earn a free ticket each.

Punctually at six, with big eating to be done, we returned
to the lighted school. Villagers with lanterns streamed in from
all quarters. We heard the bubbling of water in Barraclough's
boiler, smelt the sweet wood smoke from his fire, saw his red
face lit like a turnip lamp as he crouched to stoke up the
flames.

We lined up in the cold, not noticing the cold, waiting for

the doors to open. When they did, it was chins and boots and elbows, no queues, we just fought our way in. Lamplight and decorations had transformed the schoolroom from a prison into a banqueting hall. The long trestle-tables were patterned with food; fly-cake, brown buns, ham sandwiches. The two stoves were roaring, reeking of coke. The helpers had their teapots charged. We sat down stiffly and gazed at the food; fidgeted, coughed and waited. . . .

The stage curtains parted to reveal the Squire, wearing a cloak and a deer-stalking hat. He cast his dim, wet eyes round the crowded room, then sighed and turned to go. Somebody whispered from behind the curtain; 'Bless me!' said the Squire, and came back.

'The Parochial Church Tea!' he began, then paused. 'Is with us again . . . I suggest. And Entertainment. Another year! Another year comes round! When I see you all gathered together here – once more – when I see – when I think . . . And here you all are! When I see you here – as I'm sure you all are – once again . . . It comes to me, friends! How time – how you – how all of us here – as it were. . . .' His moustache was quivering, tears ran down his face, he groped for the curtains and left.

His place was taken by the snow-haired vicar, who beamed weakly upon us all.

'What is the smallest room in the world?' he asked.

'A mushroom!' we bawled, without hesitation.

'And the largest, may I ask?'

'ROOM FOR IMPROVEMENT!'

'You know it,' he muttered crossly. Recovering himself, he folded his hands: 'And now O bountiful Father . . . .'

We barked through grace and got our hands on the food and began to eat it any old order. Cakes, buns, ham, it didn't matter at all, we just worked from one plate to the next. Folks by the fires fanned themselves with sandwiches, a joker fried ham on the stove, steaming brown teapots passed up and down, and we were so busy there was small conversation. Through the lighted windows we could see snow falling, huge feathers against the dark. 'It's old Mother Hawkins a-plucking her geese!' cried someone: an excellent omen. Twelfth Night, and old Mother Hawkins at work, up in the sky with her birds; we loosened our belts and began to nod at each other; it was going to be a year of fat.

We had littered the tables with our messy leavings of cake crumbs and broken meat; some hands still went through the motions of eating, but clearly we'd had enough. The vicar rose to his feet again, and again we thanked the Lord. 'And now, my friends, comes the – er – feast for the soul. If you would care to – ah – take the air for a moment, willing hands are waiting to clear the hall and prepare for the – um – Entertainment. . . .'

We crowded outside and huddled in the snow while the tables were taken away. Inside, behind curtains, the actors were making up – and my moment, too, was approaching. The snow whirled about me and I began to sweat, I wanted to run off home. Then the doors reopened and I crouched by the stove, shivering and chattering with nerves. The curtains parted and the Entertainment began with a comic I neither saw nor heard. . . .

'For the next item, ladies and gentlemen, we have an instrumental duet, by Miss Brown and – er – young Laurie Lee.'

Smirking with misery I walked to the stage. Eileen's face was as white as a minim. She sat at the piano, placed the music crooked, I straightened it, it fell to the ground. I groped to retrieve it; we looked at one another with hatred; the audience was still as death. Eileen tried to give me an A, but struck B instead, and I tuned up like an ape threading needles. At last we were ready, I raised my fiddle; and Eileen was off like a

bolting horse. I caught her up in the middle of the piece —
which I believe was a lullaby — and after playing the repeats,
only twice as fast, we just stopped, frozen motionless, spent.

Some hearty stamping and whistling followed, and a shout
of 'Give us another!' Eileen and I didn't exchange a glance, but
we loved each other now. We found the music of *Danny Boy*
and began to give it all our emotion, dawdling dreamily
among the fruitier chords and scampering over the high bits;
till the audience joined in, using their hymn-singing voices,
which showed us the utmost respect. When it was over I
returned to my seat by the stove, my body feeling smooth and
beautiful. Eileen's mother was weeping into her hat, and so
was mine, I think. . . .

Now I was free to become one of the audience, and the
Entertainment burgeoned before me. What had seemed to me
earlier as the capering of demons now became a spectacle of
human genius. Turn followed turn in variety and splendour.
Mr. Crosby, the organist, told jokes and stories as though his
very life depended on them, trembling, sweating, never
pausing for a laugh, and rolling his eyes at the wings for
rescue. We loved him, however, and wouldn't let him go,
while he grew more and more hysterical, racing through
monologues, gabbling songs about shrimps, skipping, mop-
ping and jumping up and down, as though humouring a tribe
of savages.

Major Doveton came next, with his Indian banjo, which
was even harder to tune than my fiddle. He straddled a chair
and began wrestling with the keys, cursing us in English and
Urdu. Then all the strings broke, and he snarled off the stage
and began kicking the banjo round the cloakroom. He was
followed by a play in which Marjorie, as Cinderella, sat in a
goose-feathered dress in a castle. While waiting for the
pumpkin to turn into a coach she sang *All Alone By The
Telephone*.

Two ballads came next, and Mrs. Pimbury, a widow, sang them both with astonishing spirit. The first invited us to go with her to Canada; the second was addressed to a mushroom:

> Grow! Grow! Grow little mushroom grow!
> Somebody wants you soon.
> I'll call again tomorrow morning – See!
> And if you've grown bigger you will just suit ME!
> So Grow! Grow! Grow little mushroom – grow!

Though we'd not heard this before, it soon became part of our heritage, as did the song of a later lady. The last – the Baroness von Hodenburg – sealed our entertainment with almost professional distinction. She was a guest star from Sheepscombe and her appearance was striking, it enshrined all the mystery of art. She wore a loose green gown like a hospital patient's, and her hair was red and long. 'She writes,' whispered Mother. 'Poems and booklets and that.'

'I am going to sink you,' announced the lady, 'a little ditty I convected myself. Both vords und music, I may say, is mine – und zey refer to ziss pleasant valleys.'

With that she sat down, arched her beautiful back, raised her bangled wrists over the keyboard, then ripped off some startling runs and trills, and sang with a ringing laugh:

> Elfin volk come over the hill!
> Come und dance, just vere you vill!
> Brink your pipes und brink your flutes,
> Brink your sveetly soundink notes!
> Come avay-hay! Life is gay-hay!
> Life – Is – Gay!

We thought this song soppy, but we never forgot it. From then on, whenever we saw the Baroness in the lanes we used to

bawl the song at her through the hedges. But she would only stop, and cock her head, and smile dreamily to herself.

After these songs the night ended with slapstick; rough stuff about babies, chaps dressed as women, broad Gloucester exchanges between yokels and toffs, with the yokels coming off best. We ached with joy, and kicked the chairs; but we knew the end was coming. The vicar got up, proposed a vote of thanks, and said oranges would be distributed at the gate. The National Anthem was romped through, we all began coughing, then streamed outdoors through the snow.

Back home our sisters discussed their performances till the tears dripped off their noses. But to us boys it was not over, till tomorrow; there was still one squeeze left in the lemon. Tomorrow, very early, we'd go back to the schoolroom, find the baskets of broken food – half-eaten buns, ham coated with cake crumbs – and together we'd finish the lot.

A Gloucestershire village hall audience, dressed against the winter cold in 1928.

from

How To Survive
Christmas

JILLY COOPER

*Finally, a very different and contemporary view of
Christmas comes from Jilly Cooper, who was already
established as a highly successful journalist, social
commentator and writer of romantic fiction when she and
her family moved to Bisley, near Stroud, in 1982. Much
of her work up until then had centred on the lifestyle and
mores of London's smart set, but it soon became very clear
that she would find the country furrow equally productive.*

*This excerpt is from her big seller of 1986, and
doubtless many Christmases to come; we have followed
Noel and Scarlett through a succession of festive fiascos,
and as the trimmings come down for another year we find
Scarlett in pensive mood. . . .*

At home poor Scarlett is slowly ploughing through a vast
mountain of ironing, because the children all go back to school
next week. She has put the Christmas decorations back in their
box, and the tree outside the back door (it seemed such a
shame to burn it when it had given them such pleasure) and
swept up the pine needles.

She dreads taking down the Christmas cards, because it makes the sitting room look so drab and colourless. If only she hadn't spent so much on Christmas they could afford to brighten it up with new curtains, or at least new cushions. Later she's got to pack up and post back to Petersfield the gloves, boots and quilted hot-water bottle that Granny left behind, omitting to point out that Difficult Patch has punctured the hot-water bottle.

Upstairs, above the pounding surf beat of Robin's record player, she can hear Nicholas and little Carol screaming at each other. Neither can she expect any help in packing the trunks from Holly, who is locked in her room, reduced to the depths of misanthropy by mugging up St. Luke for mock O-levels.

Scarlett feels depressed. Sadly, she no longer has the excuse that it's still Christmas to justify the midday nip (a treble vodka and tonic) to keep her going; all the parties are over, and she's already broken her New Year's resolution to lose weight. Christmas, with all its faults, was a break in the monotony of life. But at least she's her own boss, unlike poor Noel, who today went back to the relentless treadmill of the office; and who now, unknown to Scarlett, is roughing it at the Ritz over a three-hour lunch with Ms. Stress, trying to piece together who it was that he mauled or insulted at the office party before Christmas.

If only, muses Scarlett, one could have Christmas every five years, then it would really be something to look forward to, like a royal wedding, and she and Noel wouldn't be almost bankrupted every January. If they could give up both drink *and* Christmas they'd be quite well off.

Her reverie is interrupted by little Carol howling down the stairs that Nicholas has decapitated her new Christmas doll, because she'd managed to wipe all his computer games.

'Never mind,' says Scarlett comfortingly. 'It's only 353 days until next Christmas.'

Acknowledgements

All unattributed items are by John Hudson, using published and unpublished reference material and personal interviews.

Both extracts from *Cider with Rosie* (1959) by Laurie Lee are reprinted by permission of the author and The Hogarth Press. 'Good King Wenceslas' by Jim Turner was first published in *Flowers From My Dustbin* (1984) and is reprinted by permission of the author. 'Under the Christmas Stars' by Humphrey Phelps was first published in *Gloucestershire and Avon Life*, December 1986, and is reprinted by permission of the author. An extract from *Cotswold Days* (Blackie, 1937) by Colin Howard. 'Robin Redbreast' by Leonard Clark was first published in *The Singing Time* (1980) and is reprinted by permission of Hodder and Stoughton Ltd. and with acknowledgement to the author's executors. Extracts from *The Season of the Year* by John Moore, first published by Collins in 1954, and from the same author's *Portrait of Elmbury*, first published by Collins in 1946, are reprinted by permission of Mrs. Lucile Bell. 'B.C.: A.D.' by U. A. Fanthorpe was first published in *Standing To* (Harry Chambers/Peterloo Poets, 1982) and is reprinted by permission of the author. 'Going A-Thomasing' by Hylda King-Ross was first published in *Gloucestershire and Avon Life*, December 1972, and is reprinted with acknowledgement to the author. 'Kiltie, The Christmas Gift Horse' by Diana Alexander is printed by permission of the author. An extract from *The Blacksmith's Daughter* by Susan Oldacre, first published by Alan Sutton in 1985, is reprinted by permission of the author. 'The School Concert' by Humphrey Phelps was first published in *Gloucestershire and Avon Life*, December 1976, and is reprinted by permission of the author. 'On Christmas Leave' by W. W. Blair-Fish was first published in *Punch*, December 27, 1916. 'Country Christmas' by Leonard Clark was first published in *Green Wood* (Max Parrish and Co. Ltd., 1962) and is reprinted with acknowledgement to the author's executors. An extract from *A Cotswold Year* by C. Henry Warren (1936). An extract from *The Diary of a Victorian Squire* by Dearman Birchall, edited by David Verey (Alan Sutton, 1983) is reprinted by permission of Mrs. Rosemary Verey. 'Christmas' by Jim Turner was first published in *Remembered Days* (1983) and is reprinted by permission of the author. 'Two Festive Recipes' by Carol Wright was first published in *Cassell's Country Cookbooks: The Cotswolds* (1975) and is reprinted by permission of Cassell and Collier Macmillan Ltd. and with acknowledgement to the author. 'A Gloucestershire Wassail' was published in this version in *Gloucestershire Notes and Queries*, Vol. IX, No. 83, 1902. An extract from *A Cotswold Village* by J. Arthur Gibbs (John Murray, 1899). 'The Oxen' by Thomas Hardy (1915). An extract from *Rural Rides of the Bristol Churchgoer* by Joseph Leech, from a reprint published by Alan Sutton in 1982. An extract from *The Glorious Glosters* by Tim Carew (Leo Cooper, 1970) is reprinted with acknowledgement to the author and publisher. 'As Hard As Winking' by Humphrey Phelps was first published in *Gloucestershire and Avon Life*, December 1983, and is reprinted by permission of the author. 'Christmas with the Mitfords' by Diana Alexander was first published in *Gloucestershire and Avon Life*, December 1980, and is reprinted by permission of the author. 'Christmas Letters from a Gloster' is an extract from *Stars in a Dark Night*, the letters of Ivor Gurney to the Chapman family, edited by Anthony Boden (Alan Sutton, 1986) and is reprinted by permission of the editor. 'The Bishop's Christmas, 1289' by David Aldred was first published in *Gloucestershire and Avon Life*, December 1984, and his 'Christmas Day in the Workhouse' in that magazine for December 1979; both are reprinted by permission of the author. 'De Spenser's Feast' by Adin Williams was first published in *Lays and Legends of Gloucestershire* (Kent/ Savory/ Davies). An extract from *Jump For Joy* by Pat Smythe, first published by Cassell and Co. (1954), is reprinted by permission of the author. 'Mum's the Word' by Michael Hardcastle was first published in *Gloucestershire and Avon Life*, December 1977, and is reprinted by permission of the author. 'The Duke of Buckingham's Christmas' by N. F. Large is published by permission of the author. 'Cold, Cold Snow' by Steven Blake was first published in *Gloucestershire and Avon Life*, December 1980, and is reprinted by permission of the author. An extract from *How To Survive Christmas* (1986) by Jilly Cooper is reprinted by permission of the author and Methuen London Ltd.

Picture credits

Page 2 top & bottom *L.P.*; 10 *B.U.P.*; 14 *G.R.O.*; 15 *Cheltenham Library*; 18 *L.P.*; 21 *Peter Jones*; 28 *L.P.*; 36 *G.R.O.*; 38 *N.F. Large*; 44 *G.R.O./Gloucester City Council*; 46 *John Purnell*; 47 *M.J. Tozer*; 54 *G.R.O.*; 59 top *L.P.*; bottom *L.P./Howard Beard*; 74 *Christopher Jordan/Emily Grove*; 79 illustration by *Phiz*; 81 *G.A.L./Brian Donnan*; 83 *June R. Lewis*; 84 *B.U.P.*; 89 *G.A.L.*; 94 *B.U.P.*; 97 *B.U.P.*; 101 *G.R.O./Thornbury Society*; 111 top & bottom *G.A.L.*; 115 *G.A.L./Pamela Jackson*; 117 *Brian Donnan*; 123 *G.A.L./Sybil Edwards*; 138 top *B.U.P.*, bottom *N.F. Large*; 139 *B.U.P.*; 140 *B.U.P.*; 144 *G.A.L./Brian Donnan*; 148 *G.R.O./Gloucester Health Authority*; 149 *Peckham's of Stroud*; 151 *N.F. Large*; 157 *G.A.L.*; 159 *L.P.*; 161 *L.P.*; 170 *Mary Trevelyan*. (Abbreviations: *L.P.* Lionel Padin; *B.U.P.* Bristol United Press; *G.R.O.* Gloucestershire County Record Office; *G.A.L.* Gloucestershire and Avon Life.)